HOW TO DRAW
TREES

FRANK M. RINES

DOVER PUBLICATIONS
Garden City, New York

Bibliographical Note

This Dover edition, first published in 2007, is an unabridged republication of the revised edition of the work, originally published by Bridgman Publishers, Inc., Pelham, N.Y., in 1946 under the title *Tree Drawing: Design and Construction*. The first edition, which appeared under the title *Design and Construction in Tree Drawing,* was published by Bridgman Publishers, Inc., Pelham, N.Y., in 1936.

Library of Congress Cataloging-in-Publication Data

Rines, Frank M.
    [Tree drawing—design and construction]
    How to draw trees / Frank M. Rines.
      p. cm.
    Originally published: Tree drawing—design and construction. Pelham, New York: Bridgman Publishers, 1946, which was a revised ed. of Design and construction in tree drawing, published in 1936.
    ISBN-13: 978-0-486-45457-3 (pbk.)
    ISBN-10: 0-486-45457-6 (pbk.)
    1. Trees in art. 2. Drawing—Technique. I. Rines, Frank M. Design and construction in tree drawing. II. Title.

NC810.R53 2007
743'.76—dc22

                                      2006052108

Printed in Canada
45457609   2025
www.doverpublications.com

FOREWORD ON TREES

When I was in Art School a fellow student remarked to me, "I don't see what you find so interesting in drawing trees—they're all alike." No statement could be farther from the truth, or show less understanding of and appreciation for nature than this. In all my experience and observation of trees I have never yet seen any two, even of the same spcies, that were just alike. Neither have I ever been able to draw two that were any more than similar in their general appearance. It is this very fact—that they differ so greatly, both as to silhouette and construction, that makes them so interesting to anyone, artist or layman, who takes the time to give them more than a passing glance.

In this presentation I am making no attempt to approach the study of trees from the view point of the botanist. Many excellent books are available on this subject, and a general knowledge from this angle is very desirable. Neither am I attempting a study of the techniques of different media.

An elaboration of the advice on tree drawing, as given in "Drawing in Lead Pencil," is the idea around which this book has been conceived. In order to do this, some examples of typical, familiar trees, both with and without foliage, are presented, together with some explanatory text. I do not show the *same* tree in both Winter and Summer, but two trees of the same species, with somewhat similar growth.

These studies of separate trees are followed by illustrations of trees in groups, or incorporated as parts of more elaborate compositions. To cover a wider field than could be done were just pencil renderings used, various media have been employed, but with the emphasis in each case upon the subject matter rather than upon the technique or tricks of the medium itself.

To be able to draw and paint trees and have them look like trees and not just strokes, or gobs of paint, is the supreme test of a landscape artist's ability. A visit to some of our art galleries will convince any one that some of the exhibitors still have much to learn in this respect.

It is just as foolish for an artist who is planning to draw or paint out of doors, to neglect to familiarize himself with the construction of trees, as it would be for a portrait painter to understand thoroughly the anatomy of the human head and its component parts with the exception, we will say, of the mouth; and then to paint a shapeless smootch of red where the mouth should be, and excuse himself by saying, "Oh well, the mouth is not important, anyway."

The examples of trees presented in the following pages might be referred to as "tree portraits." They do not show (as no one drawing or photograph could show) all the different shapes and characteristics which each particular species assumes. They do, however, attempt to illustrate some of the most dominant features of some of our best known types. In many instances, several trees of the same family are shown, because trees of the same kind differ so greatly, as has already been stated. They have been drawn with sufficient attention to detail to bring out their character.

In making compositions from nature, similar to those in the last few pages of the book, it is not desirable to depict as much detail of branches, etc., as is included in the "portraits," for the lesser details are lost in consideration of the effect of the whole.

The student must realize, nevertheless, that to be able to *leave out* details in a drawing, he must first know how these omitted details would appear. To simplify, by drawing or painting broadly, because of lack of knowledge of how the detail should be drawn, is not ART—it is merely an admittance of ignorance on the part of the person making the picture, and is as evident to the intelligent observer, as if the "artist," so-called, admitted the fact in writing.

Moreover, in tree drawing, as in pictorial representation of other objects, a comprehensive understanding of the details is necessary, for a suggestion of such detail should be introduced here and there if the the resulting picture is to contain any interest. Otherwise, the flat, insipid effect, so often seen, ensues.

If, in the following pages, I repeat some of the statements already made in the section devoted to trees in "Drawing in Lead Pencil," my excuse is that these statements are extremely important, and for that reason cannot be emphasized too often.

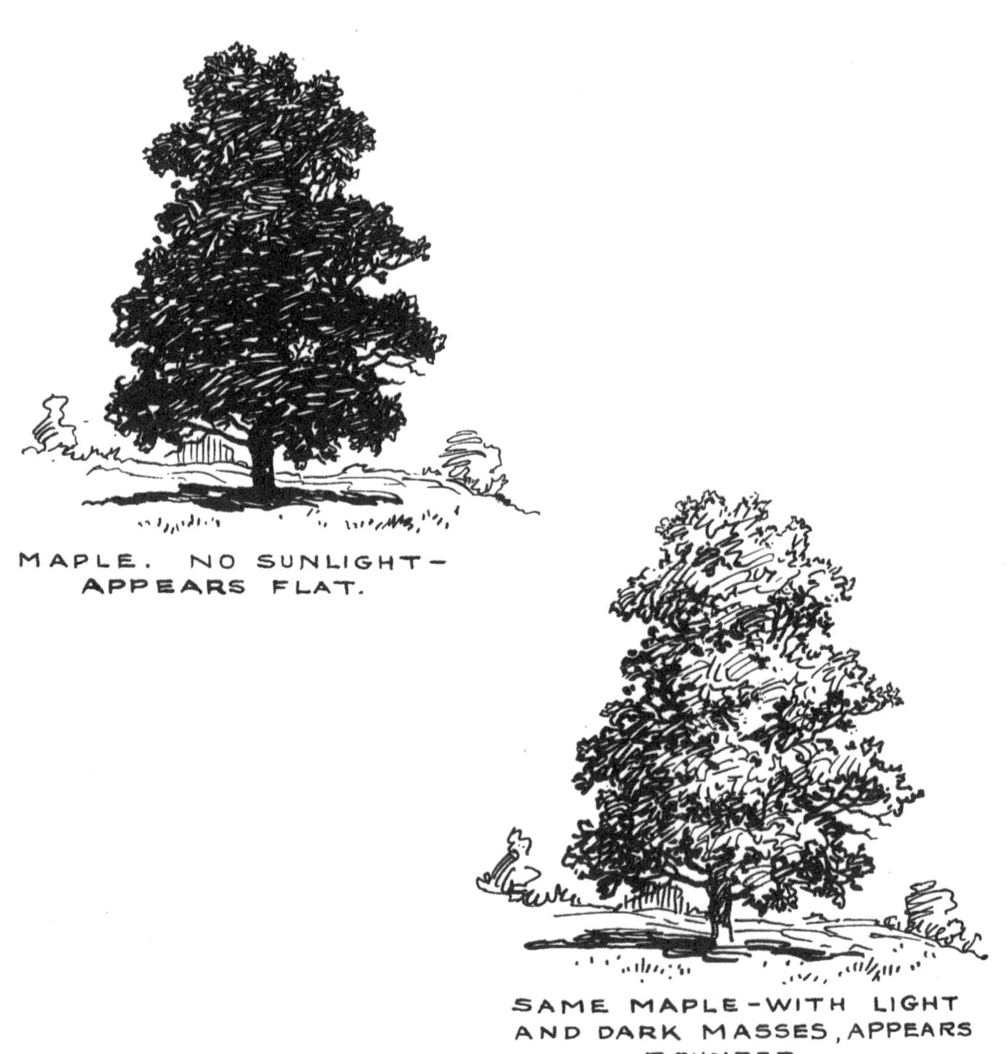

LIST OF ILLUSTRATIONS

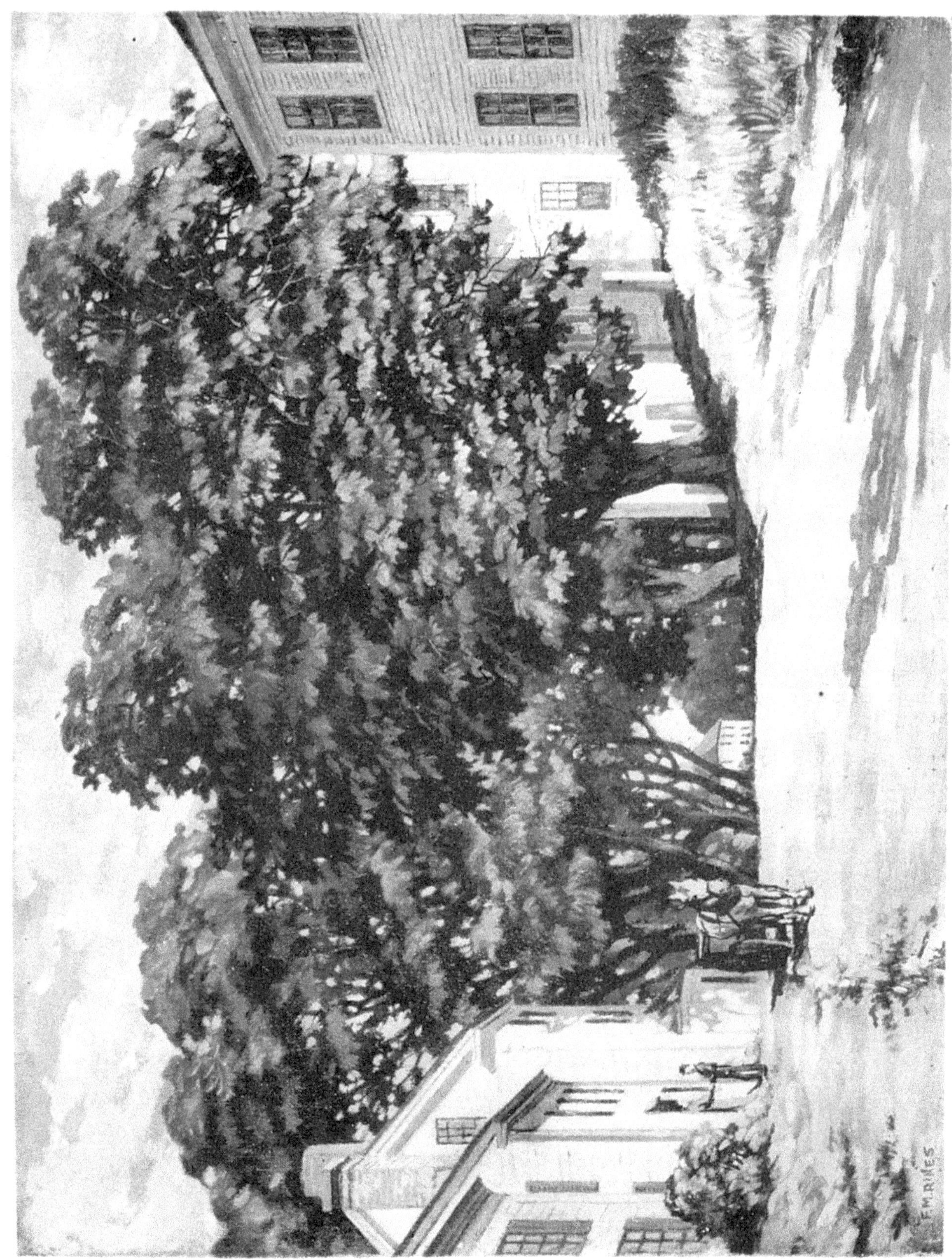

DESIGN AND CONSTRUCTION IN TREE DRAWING

One of the first things to be undertaken by anyone desirous of learning to paint and draw trees (which should include everyone intending to paint out of doors), is a constant observation and study of them—as many kinds as possible at all seasons. The student should make numerous sketches, not only of the complete trees, but of their details, especially in the Fall and Winter when, denuded of their foliage, their anatomy is so clearly revealed. Their character, as typified by the graceful branches of the elm and birch, or the ruggedness of the oak, will prove a revelation to those who have not previously paid them sufficient attention.

To illustrate this character, to impress it upon the mind of the observer of the picture, even though he may not be able to analyze it or to be consciously aware of it, should be the aim of the artist. If the artist succeeds in conveying to the observer the thought that the tree, or trees, are objects of beauty (as the artist himself should feel that they are) he has accomplished something worth while.

It is not sufficient, merely, to be a good draughtsman—to be able to draw accurately what one sees. No man, even though possessed of a "photographic eye," could draw, exactly as they are, every little branch and twig or leaf. Of course, admitting such a thing were possible, it would not be desir'able; it would not be pleasing.

Instead, the artist must be sufficiently familiar with his subject to know and appreciate the facts as they apply to the particular tree he is sketching; to be able to put down, upon paper or canvas, the dominant characteristics of the tree as they impress him. He must be able to design the limbs, branches, and twigs, and sky spaces, or the foliage masses as regards form and location, in such a manner that the unpleasant features, if any (and there usually are such), are subordinated or eliminated altogether.

Just how this shall be done depends upon several things—how important the tree is in its relation to other trees, and to the composition as a whole, and the medium employed.

Naturally, when painting in oils, the effect must be obtained differently than when using the pencil or the pen, but the idea—the principle—should be the same.

Before actually drawing a line, the tree should be studied for a few moments. Search for its outstanding features; wherein it differs from others of its kind, and yet conforms to certain rules of growth in common with the particular species to which it belongs.

Considering, first, the tree when bare of foliage or when the leaves are very sparse, sketch in the trunk and principal branches about as they appear. If, however, some of these main branches are distorted and broken, or do not form a pleasing line or pattern, change them—enough to cor'rect this unpleasant effect, still keeping the same general character of growth.

For instance, the main trunk may grow quite straight, and somewhere along this trunk two limbs may grow, one on either side, at exactly the same point. They may be of almost the same size, or thickness, and form approximately the same angle with this main stem. (See Diagram 1 E.)

Raise or lower one of these limbs a little, at the same time change the thickness and angle a bit, and note how much more pleasing is the result (2E). It might have grown this way just as well, so you will not be violating any principle, but the appearance will be more informal, and therefore more natural. Take especial care when one large branch appears partially behind another for some distance to redesign one of them a little. This will prevent the illusion of the two limbs appearing as one abnormally thick one and then suddenly diminishing to a much smaller size (Diagram D).

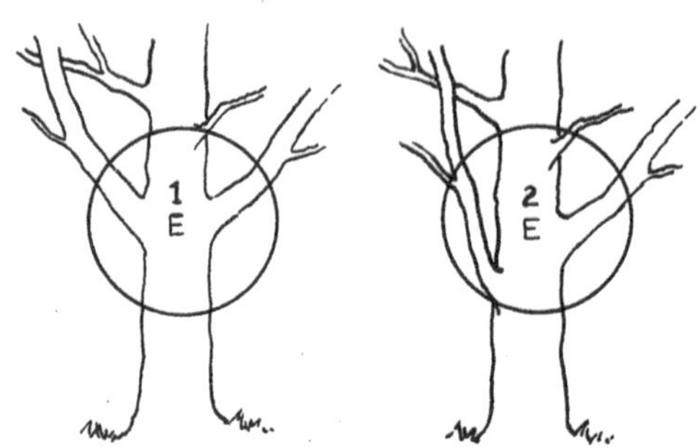

This brings up the problem of tapering the branches. This tapering must be consistent. Do not have a limb or branch first thick, then thin, and then thick again. This is not the way they grow. Neither must the branch be drawn a certain thickness for about three-fourths of its length and then suddenly be made smaller, in order to have it end where it should. (Diagram L, with arrows). This is one of the mistakes most frequently made by students when they first start to draw trees. Then they try to rectify it by running the branch off the paper, or leaving it with the appearance of having been broken off.

When the trunk and principal branches have been designed (for "designed" is exactly what they should be) commence drawing the smaller twigs. Several things should be kept in mind when drawing these twigs. The first, and most important, is to have them take on the same general character as are those of the tree which you are drawing. This may mean that they are curving and sinuous, or angular and scraggly, or both. Having, assumably, already determined this character in the preliminary study, less reference to the actual tree is now necessary, for from now on, the attention to the pattern should be uppermost. This means not only the design of the individual twigs, but of the sky spaces as well.

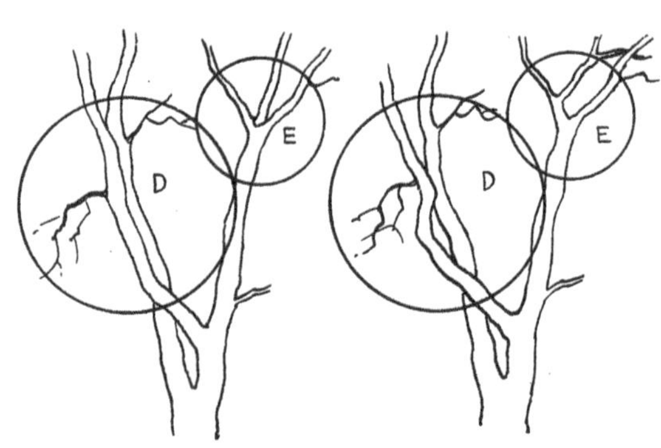

Try to get as great a variety in these twigs as possible, both in length and thickness. Just as the larger branches taper, so do the twigs. Instead of having them end with a heavy line, let them become thinner and thinner until they finally end with a hair line. (See T, in previous diagram.) Draw them crossing one another, avoid as much as possible having two or more that are too obviously parallel, and do not have a twig or branch grow at exactly the point at which two others already cross. (Diagram X.)

In some spots the twigs should be massed quite thickly, while in other places they should be comparatively more open; in the former instance the individual twigs should, more or less, lose their identity, while in the latter case some of them should be quite prominent.

When drawing these finer twigs with the pencil, pen, crayon, etc., if the instrument is allowed to twirl between the fingers now and then, a freer line results. It is also easier to get a fine line ending in this manner, and you are enabled to avoid the stiff, mechanical line obtained when holding the implement rigidly.

When you have carried your drawing to this stage, and have massed the twigs in some places more than in others, a spotty appearance around the edges will probably result. Here again, your sense of design, or pattern, must play an important part, for these spots should be made to vary as much as possible, both as to size, shape, and continuity. The same thing is true of the sky spaces;

they need to be broken up by drawing branches and twigs through them, so that no too obvious shapes result.

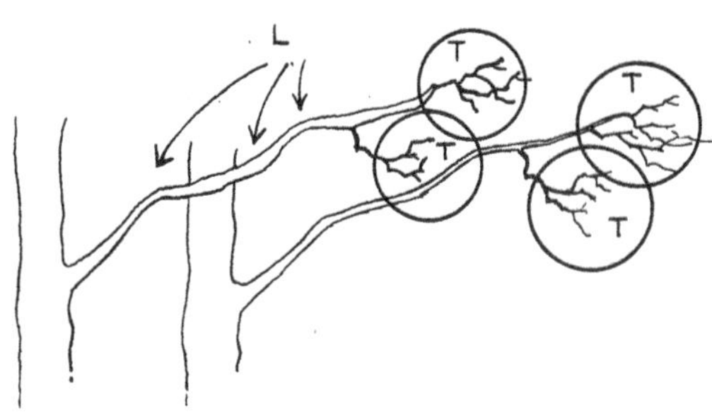

I usually make several massings of these fine twigs in different parts of the tree, at first, and then commence designing, or tying them together. In this way, I am able to get a more apparently, unstudied effect than if I were to start at any one point and continue around until I reached the starting point again.

As to just where these massings should be placed, no one can say. The artist should have a "feeling" that they should be here, or there. No two artists, drawing the same tree, would get the same spotting, and no one, drawing the same tree twice, would plan it identically each time.

A reference to the accompanying diagram will illustrate more fully some of the foregoing points. The dotted lines indicate where three limbs of equal thickness, and growing evenly spaced on the larger branch, have been changed, both in size and spacing and direction, in order to give variety to the pattern. At the same time this re-arrangement prevents the two sky spaces (S) from being so nearly similar in shape and area.

A careful study of the drawings of the trees in Winter, reproduced farther on, will help to make some of these features clearer.

Of course, many of these things which have been illustrated in the diagrams, and which I have been cautioning you to watch for, cannot be avoided unless one were to work over and over, which would utterly destroy the free, or spontaneous, effect that every sketch should possess. It is natural to overlook some of these points. However, if you have them clearly in mind, many of them can be eliminated, and the more glaring violations altered without destroying the freedom of the sketch. As a rule, this appear-ance of freedom is obtained only by a great deal of careful study and planning.

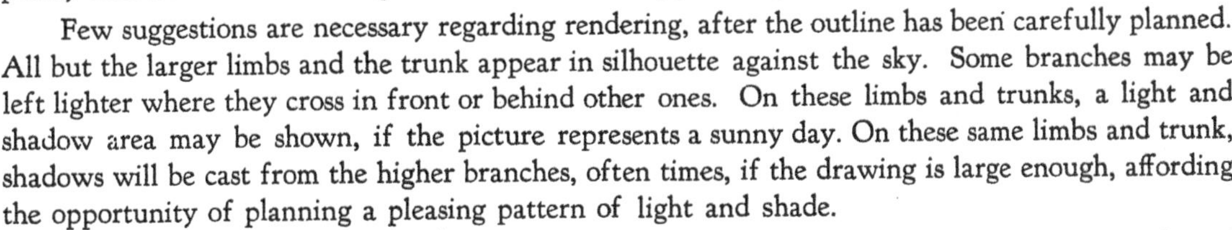

It may seem that too much importance is attached to such apparently minor things as the twig of a tree and its position. But it is these seemingly trivial things which, when the picture is viewed as a whole, are so subordinate, that make the final result successful or otherwise. Furthermore, care and skill in executing these details is not alone essential when drawing and painting bare trees; they are equally important when sketch-ing trees and bushes with foliage. An otherwise very nicely handled mass of leaves can be ruined by the introduction of poorly executed limbs and twigs. I have seen this happen frequently.

Few suggestions are necessary regarding rendering, after the outline has been carefully planned. All but the larger limbs and the trunk appear in silhouette against the sky. Some branches may be left lighter where they cross in front or behind other ones. On these limbs and trunks, a light and shadow area may be shown, if the picture represents a sunny day. On these same limbs and trunk, shadows will be cast from the higher branches, often times, if the drawing is large enough, affording the opportunity of planning a pleasing pattern of light and shade.

When drawing trees (or anything else for that matter) you should frequently stop work and

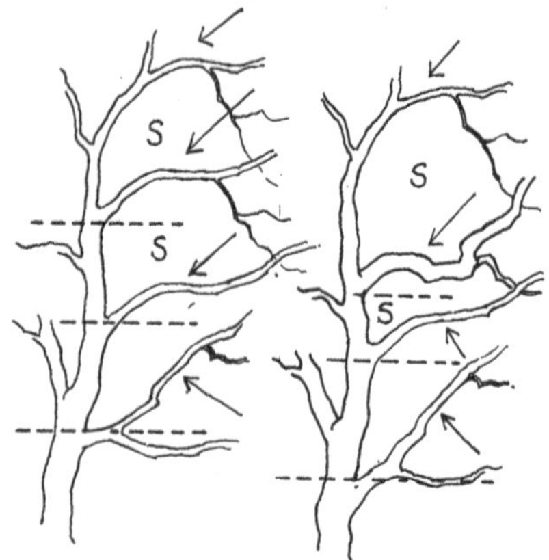

place the drawing some distance away. Relax, and look around at other objects for a few moments before studying the drawing from this distance. This rests the brain, the eye and the hand. Only by doing this can a true sense of the de-sign, or "feeling" be obtained. This very logical procedure is one of the most difficult to get students to do. It seems to them like a waste of time, but time, in the end, is actually saved, and a better picture results.

Let us now consider drawing trees in Summer, when, in full foliage, their whole appearance is so different in com-parison with Winter, when the skeletons stand out against the sky. The most noticeable feature of the tree now is its silhouette. Before the eye takes in the details of the separate foliage masses, or the branch construction, it is arrested by the shape, or outline of the tree against the sky.

This, then, should be the first thing to roughly sketch, or block in. Having already determined by a preliminary study, as previously described, the general shape of the tree—whether it is higher than it is wide, or the reverse, and roughly blocked it in, the next step is to go over this light outline, refining and changing it a little here and there. Do not be content with having, for example, three masses of foliage of about equal size and shape jutting out with equal spacing between them, either because they are like that actually, or because you happen to have drawn them that way. Shorten or lengthen one of them a trifle, make one of them thicker, thereby changing not only the size of that particular clump, but at the same time altering the separating spaces.

Do not, above all things, be satisfied to complete the outline with three or four curving strokes that make it appear like something cut out from a plank or piece of wall board with a jig-saw. This may sound far-fetched, and yet I have seen it done many times, not only by students, but by professionals.

Remember the foliage is something through which the wind can blow, causing the leaves to tremble and rustle; there-fore, indicate in the outline the soft and lace-like edges. Handle this outline in such a manner as to suggest the abovementioned quality and to create the impression that it is different material from the buildings, rocks, boats, etc., that may also be in the com-position. (See accompanying diagram.)

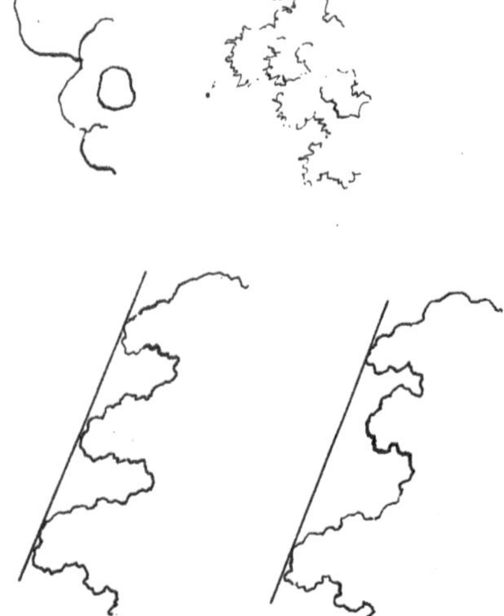

Another thing to bear in mind is that all trees have three dimensions—that they have *depth* as well as height and breadth. So many times they are drawn and painted as if they were flat, like a piece of paper. Usually in photographs, also, they have the appearance of being all one tone, with little or no modeling in them. In the case of the photograph this effect is due to either one or both of two things; the film is not sensitive to the different color values, or else the picture was taken with the sun behind the tree.

But we, as artists, should be able to improve upon the camera. There are several means by which we can do this. One way is by changing and redesigning, as already described (and to be emphasized further), and another way is by selecting the point from which we view our subjects so that the light comes from some other angle than directly in front of us, thereby throwing sunlight and consequently shadow upon the objects.

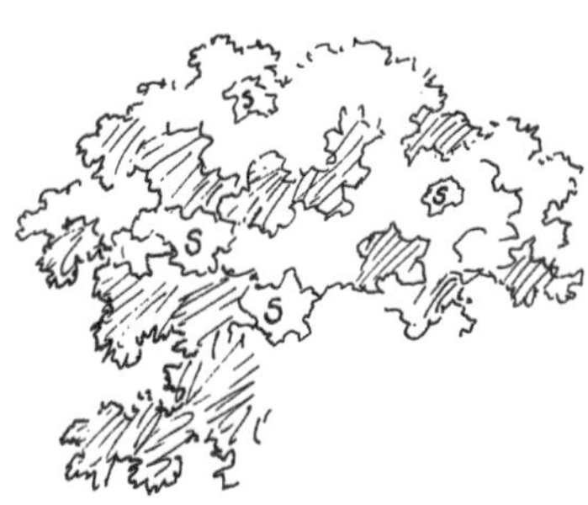

It is this contrast of both light and shade that makes a picture interesting. This is equally as true of trees as it is of buildings, rocks, boats, etc. Of course, there are exceptions to this rule. Sometimes we wish to paint gray day effects and so on, but generally speaking, it is the sunny effects that are most pleasing especially when working in black and white.

All of which leads us to the next stage in making the tree outline, after the general silhouette has been drawn.

In the same manner with which you have blocked in the outer edge, draw the shapes of the light and dark masses of foliage, and the largest, or principal, skyholes. If the foliage is open enough so that the large branches show, sketch them also. Do not bother to draw the smaller twigs, except to indicate where a cluster may show.

The drawing will now have the appearance of a more or less confining outline, enclosing a lot of meaningless lines—there will be no distinction between the foliage masses and the skyholes. A helpful idea is to make, very lightly, a small letter "s" in these sky spaces, and to "scumble" in a few lines to denote the areas that are to be in shadow. (See diagram.)

The result now is what might be termed a rough diagram of the tree. The lines should, of course, be kept light so they will not show when the rendering is completed.

Now, surely, you are ready to start the tone, or color, it would seem. But there is yet one more step to be taken before facing this final problem. It is—to study the pattern of these masses and their confining outline once more.

Does the whole silhouette have the appearance of informal balance? Are the different masses varied enough as to size, shape, and continuity? Are they distributed in such a manner that the tree does not have the effect of being divided right through the center in respect to the light and shade areas? Are the skyholes sufficiently varied in character so as not to seem made with a rubber stamp?

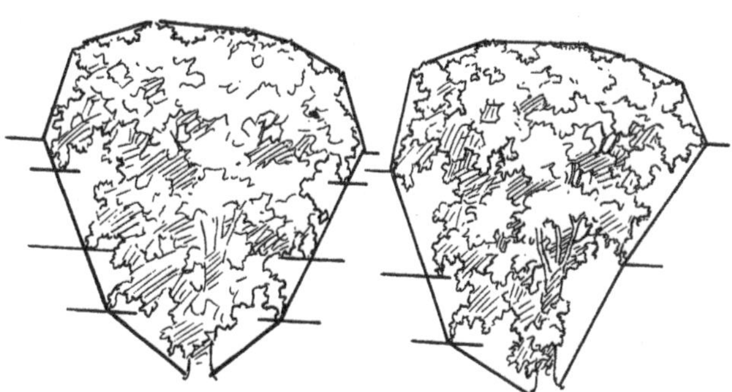

If the answer to any of these questions is "no," then now is the time for alterations; now is the time to correct these faults.

Most of you who read this will be much surprised, no doubt, to find that so much time and effort should be devoted to merely the outline of a tree; something that eventually will be covered up. But this is exactly the secret of being able to draw a tree well. The additional time required to follow out the preceding stages is time and labor saved later on and is the only way by which satisfactory results can be obtained. All this work, as well as that to follow, is bound to require time at first. As the student progresses, and increases his skill by more and more practice, less time is required to perform this preliminary work, and yet it should never be neglected.

In applying the tones, shading, color, or whatever term may be given a filling in the outline, a feeling for the *direction* of the leaf growth and the leaf massing must be evident. This is true, to a greater or less extent, no matter what medium is employed. When using the pencil or pen and ink, crayon, etc., the strokes should be more defined than when using, for instance, oils—for both the pencil and the pen require plenty of "technique" if they are to show to their greatest advantage. Even in using the other media, however, the tones should be applied in such a manner that a suggestion of the texture is given; otherwise the result will not appear as foliage.

In every tree, as we must have discovered in our study of the bare trees, the tendency is for the topmost twigs to grow in a more or less vertical direction. In some species, as well as in some individual trees, this direction is more evident than in others, but it always exists to some degree.

Once we get away from the top, however, the change of direction of growth differs considerably. Compare, for example, the elm and the maple and the oak. (See diagrams.)

A more thorough realization of these differences will be obtained by reference to the following "tree portraits" and to the real trees. The previous practice of drawing bare trees should also help to emphasize this very important characteristic.

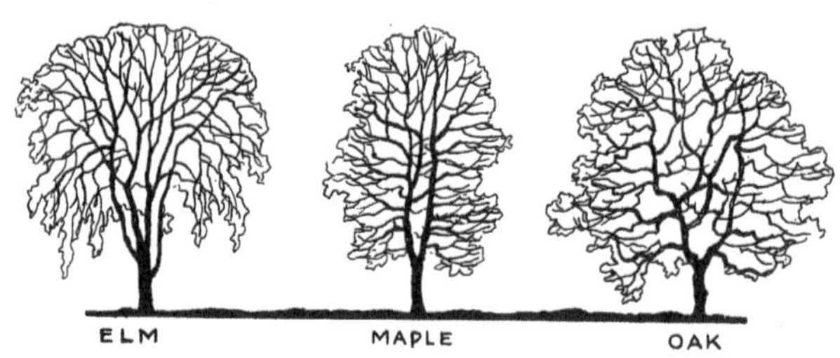

Our strokes, then, should be made with these directions of growth in mind—especially around the edges, or silhouette, of the tree. When leaving the edges, and working toward the interior, the strokes should vary more, for the masses now are extending in several different directions, with some reaching out almost directly toward you, and others shooting off at various angles It is, therefore, along the edges that the greatest effort to express the character should be brought to bear.

Try the following experiment, which will demonstrate the preceding paragraph clearly.

Make a small hole about one-half inch in diameter in the center of a piece of paper. Holding this near one eye, with the other eye closed, look at the middle of a mass of foliage (either in nature or a photograph). Nothing but a spot will appear; it might be anything or nothing at all. Now move the paper so that part of the edge of the foliage against the sky shows through the hole. Immediately the fact that you are looking at a tree becomes apparent. Now try the same test with any of the sketches in this book. This proves that it is the *silhouette* that determines the character of the tree. Notice the difference between the edges of various kinds of foliage. See how logical it is to bring out this difference in your drawing.

If we have been careful to select a tree upon which the sun casts both light and shadow, it will be seen that the *values* of the foliage masses vary greatly. Emphasize these variations in your drawing even to the extent of exaggeration, if necessary, in order to produce the required sunny effect.

Exaggerate, also, the sharpness of the edges of the light and dark masses of foliage as you work away from the outer contour, especially when drawing in black and white. It is better to get more contrast and sharper edges to these forms than it is to get not enough, for these separations can be softened or blended more easily than they can be sharpened. When working in black and white, many of the sunlit areas should be left as pure white paper; therefore, take care to leave plenty of white space, or else you will find that when the edges have been softened, in places, by working from the dark tones into the light, that the white paper has suddenly disappeared altogether. In color, of course, these same light parts will need light washes on them.

[14]

The best procedure for a while, after the outline or diagram, as previously described, has been planned, is to work in all the dark areas first, and then add the lighter tones, but after sufficient experience, the best results are obtained by introducing the several tones at the same time.

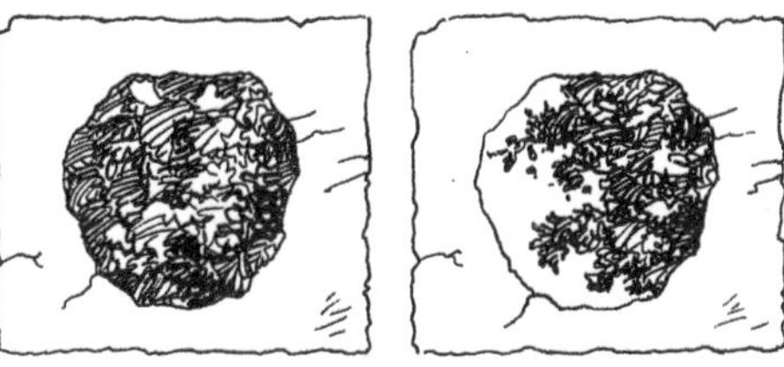

Too much stress cannot be placed upon the importance of these masses. They are what cause the tree to appear round, or three dimensional, as well as giving the impression of sunlight. How frequently we see compositions in which everything but the foliage (the houses, rocks, etc.) have light and shadow on them while the foliage itself suggests the idea of a cloudy day.

These masses of light and dark are often very subtle, however. They are not always clearly defined or easily distinguishable; and, as in the case of the branches of the trees in Winter, they do not always arrange themselves just as we may wish to have them. So once again, our sense of design must be called upon, to enable us to rearrange them as regards position, size, and form.

Just as you should avoid several masses along the edge forming too definite a straight line, just so should you also avoid two or more of these light or dark bunches forming a pattern that is too obvious. Just as you should introduce twigs and branches when drawing bare trees, in order to break up what would otherwise be too uniform spaces between the larger limbs, so too, should these light and dark masses be broken up, in order to avoid the monotony of equality of size and contour.

But, you will say, I've already taken care of these patterns when drawing the outline, before I commenced to render. Very true; but as you will see for yourself, the pattern appears quite different now. It is almost impossible to plan every little area, in outline, just as it should finally be. The outline, at best, is a guide to only the larger masses; the feeling for pattern must dominate during the entire rendering. Do not hesitate to change the original plans wherever it seems necessary.

We have now reached the point where we have a more or less interesting group of tones, or strokes, but it still doesn't quite look like a tree—something is lacking. What is needed now, to pull the whole mass together and have it appear as it should, is, of course, the trunk, branches and twigs. These should purposely be left until the last .

In some types of trees, as well as in different trees, the "anatomy" is more evident than in others. All trees, however, unless, of course, they are very much in mass in the background, are improved a great deal if some of the branch structure is shown.

Instead of drawing these branches definitely in the beginning, and then having to design the foliage to grow from them, it is much better to draw them now—not necessarily in just the same locations as they are actually, but where they seem to be needed to support a clump of foliage as you have placed it.

The lighter bunches of foliage indicated a sufficiently thick growth of leaves to catch the sunlight and for the most part are extending toward you, or in front of the trunk; therefore, the twigs and branches would not be seen in these areas. They would be mostly in evidence in the skyholes, in silhouette, and oftentimes showing lighter against a mass in shadow. Drawing them in these skyholes also helps to differentiate between the sky spaces and the lighter foliage tones, especially when these lighter tones are represented by white paper. Sometimes a dead limb or twig projecting beyond the edge is effective.

To know just how many or how few of these branches to show is important; it depends, to a great degrees, upon other parts of the picture, and, of course, upon the medium used. A sufficient number to suggest the construction of the tree—to give it "character," should be drawn, in any event.

Before calling the drawing finished, one more step is necessary. Although, throughout the process up to now, we have watched very carefully the design of the edges, the massing and the sky spaces, and have improved upon our original pattern as we have progressed, we must now study the whole design, as one unit, in the same manner as described for the Winter trees, that is, by getting away from it, and viewing it, first, as a whole and then as regards its individual characteristics.

A touch here, an accent there, a subtle connection between two spots, that stand out too prominently, will make the difference between something mediocre and something really good.

By this time, if not before, you have, I hope, become convinced of the importance of DESIGN in its relation to tree representation.

It is a pretty generally accepted fact that an artist, when starting to paint an outdoor subject, should not attempt to picture everything exactly as it is. If that is the idea—to show everything as it exists—the camera can do a much better job of it than any artist, no matter how clever he may be. Especially is this true since color photography has been developed to its present stage.

The camera *must* show things exactly as they are—being a piece of mechanism, it has no brain, and therefore, no sense of discrimination.

The artist does not hesitate to leave out and rearrange or transpose objects in order to produce what according to his ideas will make a better picture. "Yes," you say, "but that is 'composition,' isn't it?" Exactly! The words "design" and "pattern" which I have used so frequently throughout the preceding pages are synonymous with the term "composition." They mean one and the same thing.

If the composition of the whole scene should be so carefully planned with the object of producing a pleasing effect, should not the composition of the separate units of which the whole is composed receive equal consideration? If it is desirable to leave out a telegraph pole, or a billboard, because they would form a discordant note, is it not equally logical to eliminate an unfortunate shape, in the tree or foliage, which are a part of the whole composition?

Merely to draw or paint a tree so that one can tell it is a tree is quite simple—to be able to represent a tree that looks like a tree and is well designed also, is a more difficult and yet a well worth while undertaking.

The greater part of what I have said so far applies specifically, to drawing a tree when it is considered as a unit or a portrait of a tree. To the student who is desirous of doing landscape subjects, and doing them well, a great amount of time and practice should be devoted to this work. When it comes to depicting groups of trees against backgrounds of buildings, etc., and more or less merging with each other, the same principles should be applied, except that in many cases some of the foliage should be somewhat simplified. While less detail should be shown, or not emphasized so much, that which is presented should be given sufficient attention to warrant its inclusion.

A reference to the compositions in the back of the book will, I hope, make this evident.

When it is not possible to go out of doors and sketch, the next best thing is to work from photographs, either those you have made yourself or as found in magazines. Do not attempt to "copy" them, any more than if you were drawing directly from nature. Regard them as so much data from which to build your own "story" or composition.

Although, as I have stated in the foreword the technique of different media is not to be emphasized, a few words on the subject should prove helpful.

Of all the many media which are possible to use, and which are interesting to experiment with, the pencil is by far the most satisfactory for students use, especially when working out of doors. Notice that I do not say it is the "easiest," for, contrary to popular belief, it is not so simple a medium when properly handled. However, once you learn to use the pencil intelligently, and can make a good drawing with it, you will have very little difficulty in using any of the other black and white media. Its proper use involves the solving of every problem which the other tools present only in part.

The better makes of drawing pencils, of which there are several, are made in a series of seventeen degrees of hardness and softness. They range from 9H (hard) to 6B (soft, or black). For our purposes the 2H, H, F, HB, B, 2B, 3B, and 4B are all that is necessary, but none of these grades should be omitted.

There is only one kind of paper which will produce the crisp tones so essential to a really good pencil sketch. It is the "Strathmore" *smooth* finish Bristol Board. All the pencil drawings reproduced in this book were made on this paper; in fact, I use no other, and I insist upon all my students using it. If you ask for it by name, it should be obtainable in any artist's supply store.

In order to get the best results with the pencils, they must, like any other tools, be handled properly. With the exception of the one used for the outline drawing (an F or an H) the other pencils should be first sharpened with a rather stubby point and then beveled, on one side only, on a piece of fine sandpaper or similar abrasive material to an angle of about $45°$. This angle may vary somewhat with different individuals—experiment a little until you get the right angle to correspond with the angle at which you naturally hold the pencil when writing, thereby avoiding an awkward or unnatural position of your hand.

When the pencils have all been carefully sharpened in this manner, the pencil strokes should be applied with a very firm pressure. Do not bear down heavily and then lightly with the same pencil to get different tones, but change the pencils as often as a different value is desired, pressing firmly at all times. This method will produce crisp, clean effects; the one-pencil, varying pressure method will produce a fuzzy uncertain appearance.

The direction of the strokes should be governed by the contour and texture of the material to be represented. Foliage, for the most part, should be rendered with short curving strokes, sometimes open and separated, and again overlapping and massed. Try to express the feeling for the direction of the strokes as suggested by the actual object, or material.

The foregoing method of applying the strokes should be done with the flat edge of the pencil. When indicating fine twigs and sharp accents, etc., the pencil may be turned edgewise and a fine sharp line may be obtained. Great care should be taken to keep the beveled edges in their proper condition, by frequent use of the sandpaper; otherwise, several different bevels, like the facets of a diamond, will tend towards narrower strokes.

When necessary to change the value of an area already rendered, *do not* go over it with a softer pencil. To do so will destroy all the crispness and freshness. Lift off, first, with a piece of Kneaded Eraser (obtainable at all art and most stationery stores) as much of the tone as possible; then erase, completely if possible, with an ordinary red eraser, the remaining tone. Finally, render this area again, using the pencil you should have originally used.

When a pencil drawing is made with the proper pencils on the proper paper in the manner

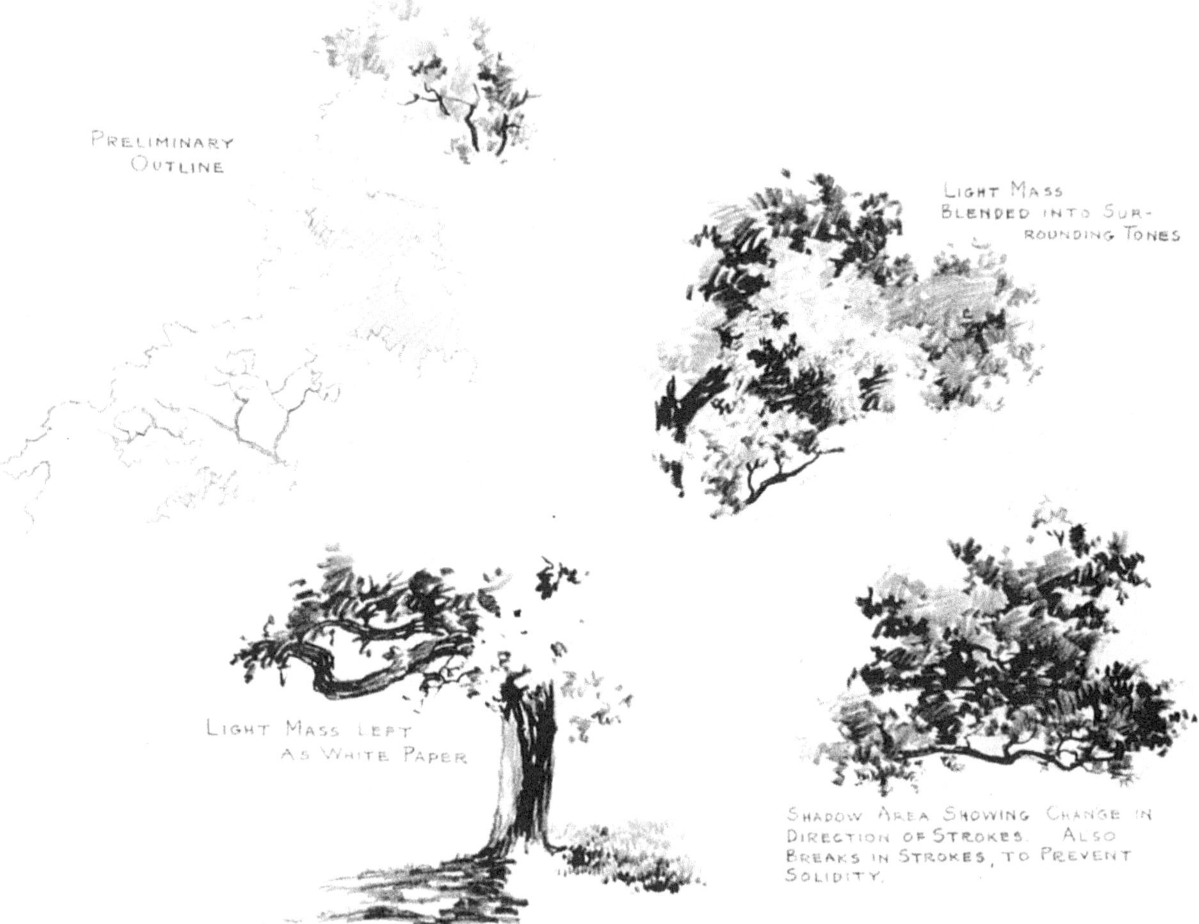

described, no "fixatif" is needed to protect it from smudging. A piece of smooth paper, fastened at the top edge and forming a flap, will give ample protection.

I usually use the same paper for pen and ink work, although many artists prefer the "medium" surfaced, manufactured by the same company. With either paper, the procedure is the same.

Unlike the pencil drawing, where a number of different pencils and only one pressure is used, I use but one pen and apply a varying pressure. The pen that I use is a Gillott Crowquill No. 303 and a waterproof black India Ink. There are several good makes obtainable.

Sufficient planning of outline and tones should precede the application of the ink, for it is extremely difficult to make alterations, should you change your mind, after a partial rendering.

While there are any number of "trick" techniques possible with the pen, it is most logical, I believe, to adhere, for a while at least, to an honest and straightforward representation. When sufficient facility is acquired, various experiments may be tried.

In the pen and ink drawings reproduced in this book, I have used the same principles to govern the direction of the strokes as those already described in making pencil sketches. The great difference is that the pen is a pointed instrument in contrast to the broader pencil "point" and therefore the finer lines which it produces must be handled with a great degree of care and skill when used to form masses. As previously mentioned, varying pressure spreads the pen point to different widths; consequently, difference in the width of line can be made, but this width does not vary as greatly as those produced with the pencil.

Care must be taken to have the pen lines sure and definite, not fuzzy and shaky.

Avoid any more changes than are absolutely necessary (hence the carefully planned pencil outline, which can be erased with a piece of soft Art Gum when the rendering is completed). When an alteration must be made, use a sharp knife or razor blade, held edgewise, partially to scratch out the line, followed by a vigorous application of hard red eraser (not ink eraser). If this is done carefully and patiently, the paper will not be roughened enough to destroy its surface. If the surface appears a bit too rough, however, the finger nail or some similar material will burnish it and further restore the original texture. Very often, in making pen drawings for reproduction, chinese or opaque white water color is used to obliterate some of the lines. When the drawing is photographed, this white paint will not show. It is best, however, to use this method very sparingly, otherwise it is easy to form a careless habit of depending upon the white paint too much.

The samples of wash drawings shown here were made by what might be termed a "building up" process. After making a careful but light pencil outline, on a fairly rough, or "cold pressed" watercolor paper, gradually strengthened washes or "coats" of charcoal gray watercolor were applied, until the drawing was built up to the desired tone. After the first light wash was put on the pencil lines were erased with Kneaded Eraser, or Art Gum. Unlike the pencil sketches, where the proper value must be put down directly, the washes gradually approach the final effect. Do not apply the next tone until the previous tone is dry, or nearly so, otherwise the drawing or modeling will get out of your control. While the brush strokes are not nearly as evident as are either the pencil or pen strokes, a sense of their direction must be retained if the result is to express any character.

The final accents should be made with practically the pure pigment, using sufficient water to allow it blending with the other tones. A fairly large brush of good quality may be used for the large washes, with a smaller one for the branches and twigs.

Lamp black or Ivory black is often used instead of the Charcoal Gray, and some interesting results may be obtained by experimenting with other colors, such as Burnt Sienna, etc.

Carbon crayon or pencil is, as the name implies, carbon in pencil form. While it does not erase so easily, nor produce the variety of tones (it comes in 3B, 2B and H) that the graphite pencils give, some interesting effects can be obtained with it. The method of making the strokes is similar to that already described for the graphite pencils. The best paper to use is the medium surfaced Strathmore mentioned for use with pen and ink, or Illustration Board.

Lithograph Crayon is a grease crayon which comes in stick form, the sticks being about $2\frac{1}{4}$ inches long by $\frac{1}{4}$ inch square. It also comes in pencil form, with a paper casing. It works very nicely on a variety of rough surfaced papers, including watercolor paper. It is extremely difficult to erase or scratch out. As in wash drawing, the strokes appear very much subordinated to the light and shade, or spotting.

The use of charcoal may, I believe, be quickly passed over, as almost everyone with any drawing training at all has used this medium to some extent. Charcoal comes in three grades; hard, medium and soft. I prefer the medium. A great variety of colors of charcoal papers are available at a very low price. It is interesting to experiment with some of these colors and to use white chalk or crayon to bring out the highlights.

One admirable feature of charcoal is its easy erasing qualities. A touch of the thumb now and then to blend some of the tones, and afterwards a touch or two of the Kneaded Eraser produces some characteristic effects.

Charcoal drawings, as well as those made with the carbon crayon, should always be sprayed with charcoal "fixatif" to prevent smudging. If the white chalk is used, the drawing should first be "fixed" before applying the chalk.

Dry brush drawings are made with the black India Ink (designated for pen and ink work) applied with a brush which is first dipped into the ink bottle and then jabbed on a blotter until more or less of the surplus ink is absorbed. The brush is then dragged over the paper, leaving, in some spots, a more or less solid black, and in other places an effect resembling stippling. If, together with these dragged-in areas, resulting from the foregoing process, patches of the full strength liquid ink are used, some very interesting results often occur. Needless to say, a very definite idea of the spotting must first be worked out.

Since working with pastels, as well as oils and water color, requires a knowledge of color in addition to drawing, tree anatomy, composition and values which are so necessary to working with any of the black and white media, the student cannot be cautioned too strongly to devote plenty of time to drawing before attempting color work. To the student who feels himself sufficiently grounded in the fundamentals of black and white to experiment with color as well as those who are already launched in this field, pastels will prove themselves fully as interesting and satisfactory as the more generally used media, i.e., oil and water color.

There are several different surfaces of pastel paper and board on the market. Those with either a "velvet" finish or sandpaper surface are excellent. The best pastels used to come from France and Germany but those made now in this country are very good.

As they are soft and break easily they are rather expensive to use. They can, however, be used up to the very smallest piece—half the size of your little finger nail. Some artists deliberately break a new stick into several pieces before using it. Such a procedure is hardly necessary though, for I find they break quickly enough anyway.

The same idea of strokes as in the pencil drawings should be maintained. While they will not be as evident in the final result, yet their influence should be felt. Except for a few details, the broad sides of the broken pieces can be used. If the texture of the surface is very rough, it may be necessary to rub in the first tones with the fingers in order to get a sufficiently covered surface upon which to build the final colors. This holds true especially for the sky. Don't rub any more than you have to, however, for the finished appearance does not want to be too "slick". By experimenting a while many tricks of handling will be discovered.

So far as I know there is no satisfactory "pastel fixatif" obtainable. The best way, when you have finished your pastel painting is to put it under glass. By so doing, it can then be handled with reasonable precaution.

Contrary to the opinion of a great many people, including unfortunately many artists, a lot of pigment, even when the color scheme is carefully planned, will NOT cover up bad drawing or the lack of good drawing. Rather will it produce the opposite effect—it will emphasize such carelessness. When painting in oils especially, many painters give all their thought to color with little or none to the things which we have been stressing here. The effect of such a picture can be compared to the impression created by a lecturer who centers all his efforts on his choice of English—on the words and phrases he uses—with practically no thought given to his subject matter.

To attempt a treatise on oil painting in the little space available here would be worse than useless. For those readers who are doing, or intend to do work in this most interesting medium, and also to those who are in touch with the exhibitions of such paintings, the best advice I know is not to let yourself be "carried away" by color but to search more deeply for the other important elements.

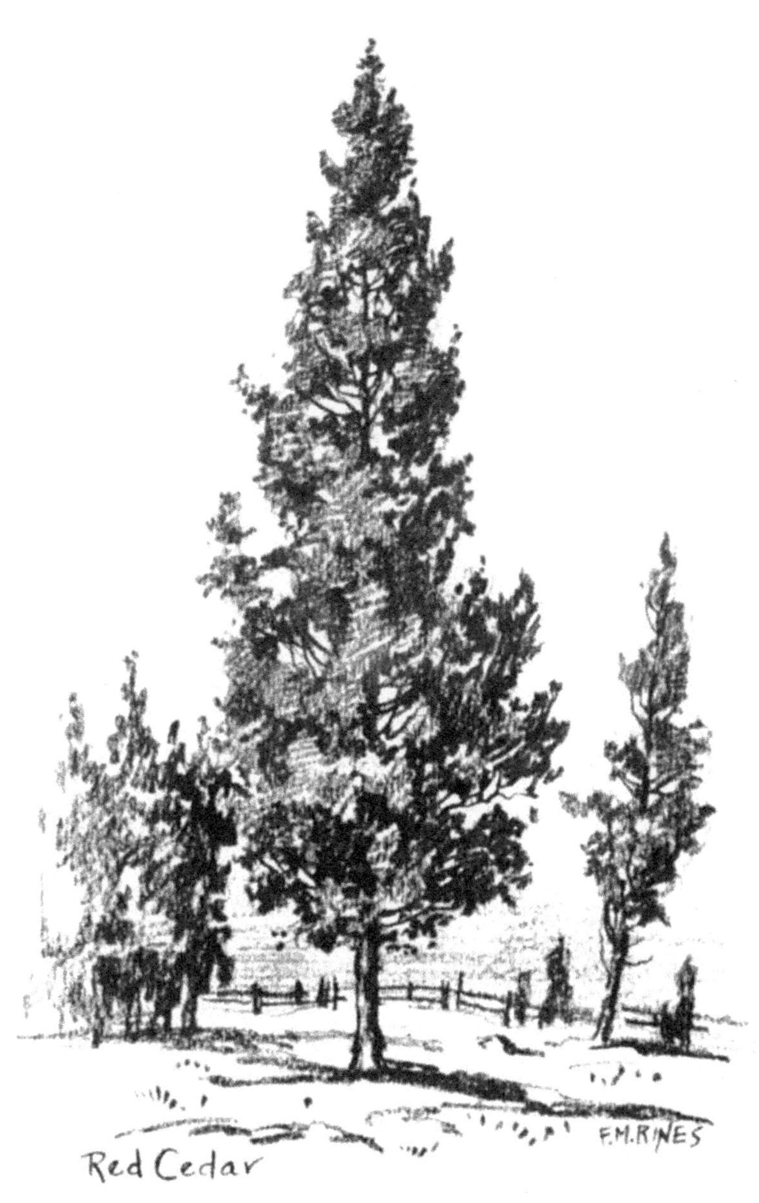

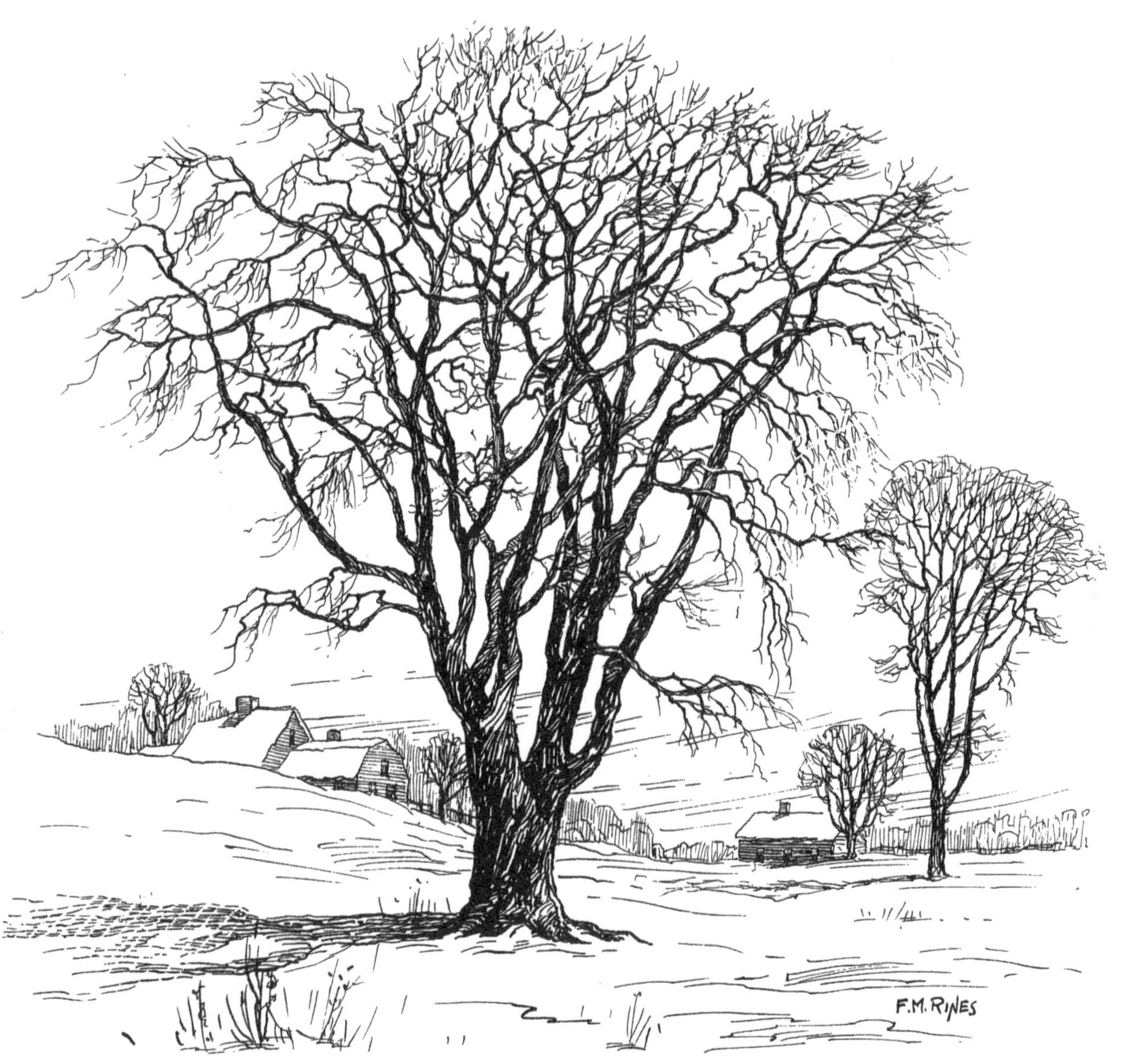

ELM. *Medium — Pen and Ink*. No tree varies more in general aspect than the elm. A semblance to the vase is the form most often assumed, when, standing in open ground, it is left free to follow its inclinations. The main trunk is frequently reinforced in old trees by huge buttresses, and often rises entire from ten to twenty feet, separating at length into several nearly equal branches. These rise, diverging but slightly, in straight lines or in broad curves, for thirty or forty feet farther, eventually sweeping outward in wide and lofty arches, with a pendant border of terminal twigs.

The greatest width, as a rule, is near the top. In some elms the branches are quite sinuous, crossing and intertwining.

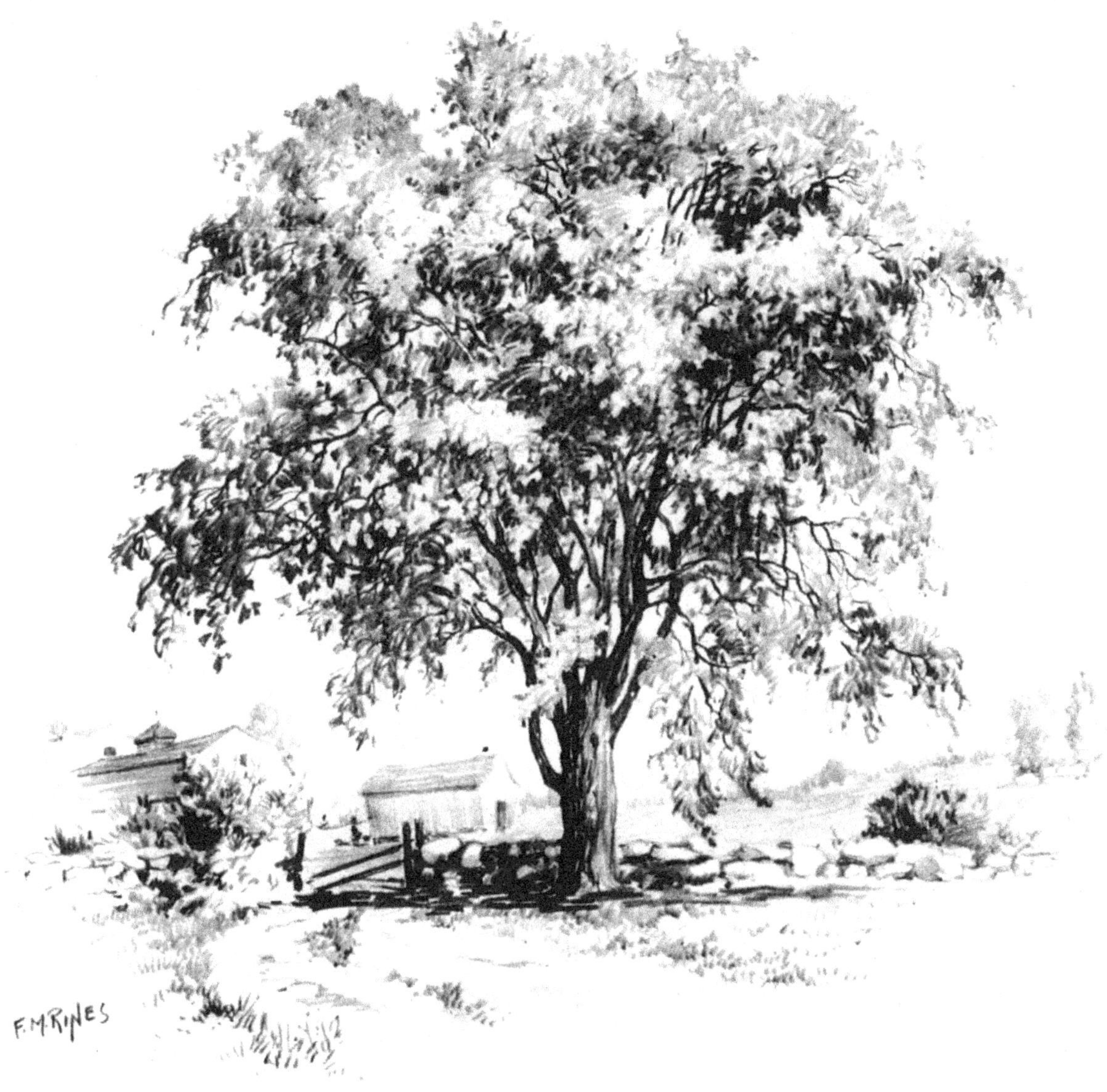

ELM. *Medium — Pencil.* The elm is one of our most widely distributed as well as most graceful trees. Although the leaves are medium sized, the many fine twigs produce definite masses, which catch the sunlight and consequently cast contrasting shadows. The weight of the foliage causes the finer branches to droop even more than when the tree is bare; therefore, the pendulous masses are very evident, especially in the lower part of the tree. The silhouette is often rather flat at the top, with sufficient open spaces to show sky and branches. Elms frequently appear like the smaller tree in the Winter sketch — tall and narrow, instead of spreading, but with the same characteristics of twigs and foliage massing.

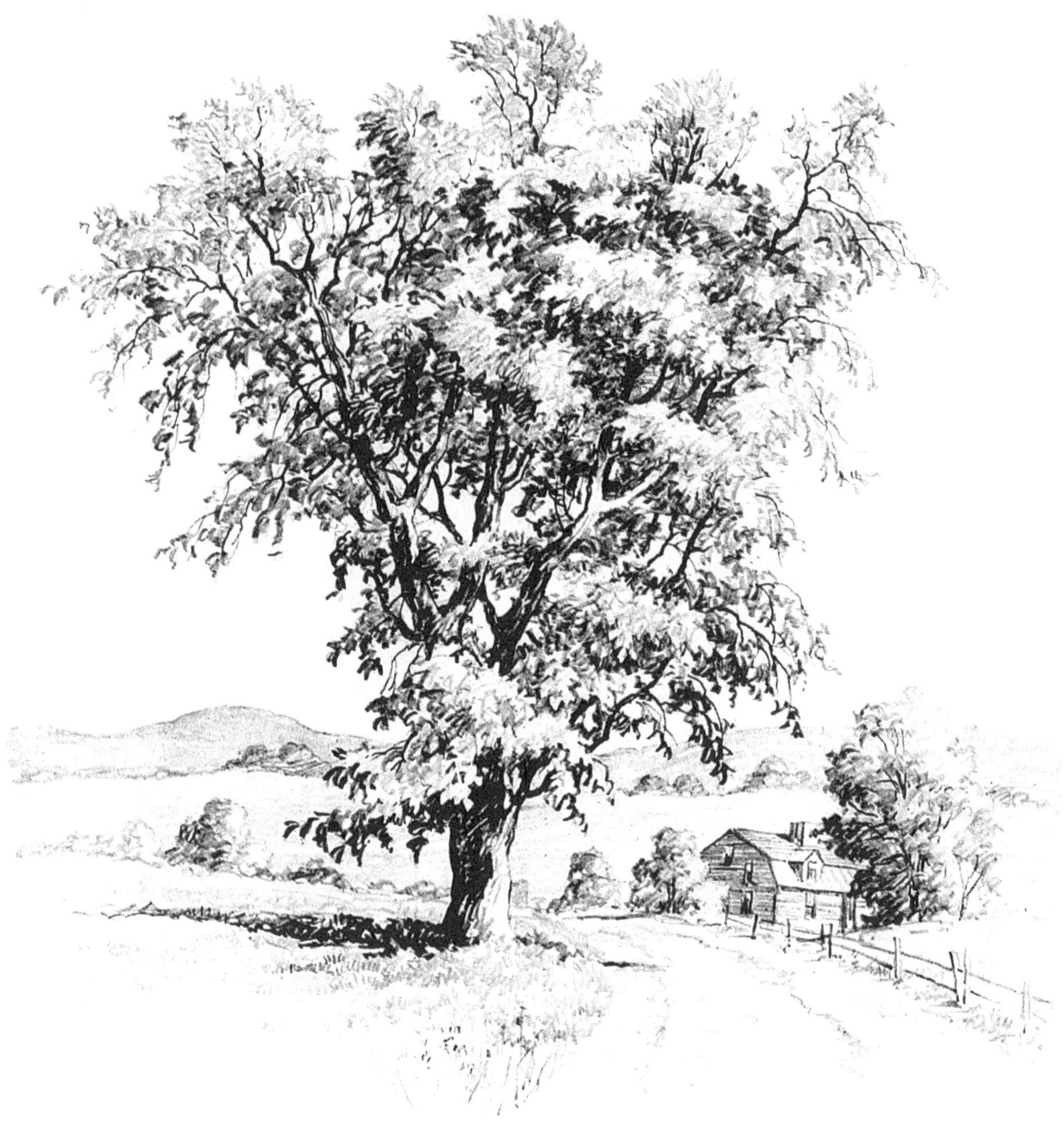

ELM. *Medium — Pencil.* A comparison of this elm tree with the one on the preceeding page, and also with the other elms shown throughout the book, demonstrates what has already been said — that no two trees are ever alike, even though they possess many similar characteristics. One of the most outstanding features of the American elm (all those in this book belong to the American grouping of the family) is the pendulous branches, especially the lower ones.

In drawing these, take care not to make them look like bunches of grapes hanging straight down as if there were no life in them. Note how they vary in direction and how, nearly always, there is a tendency toward an outward or upward direction.

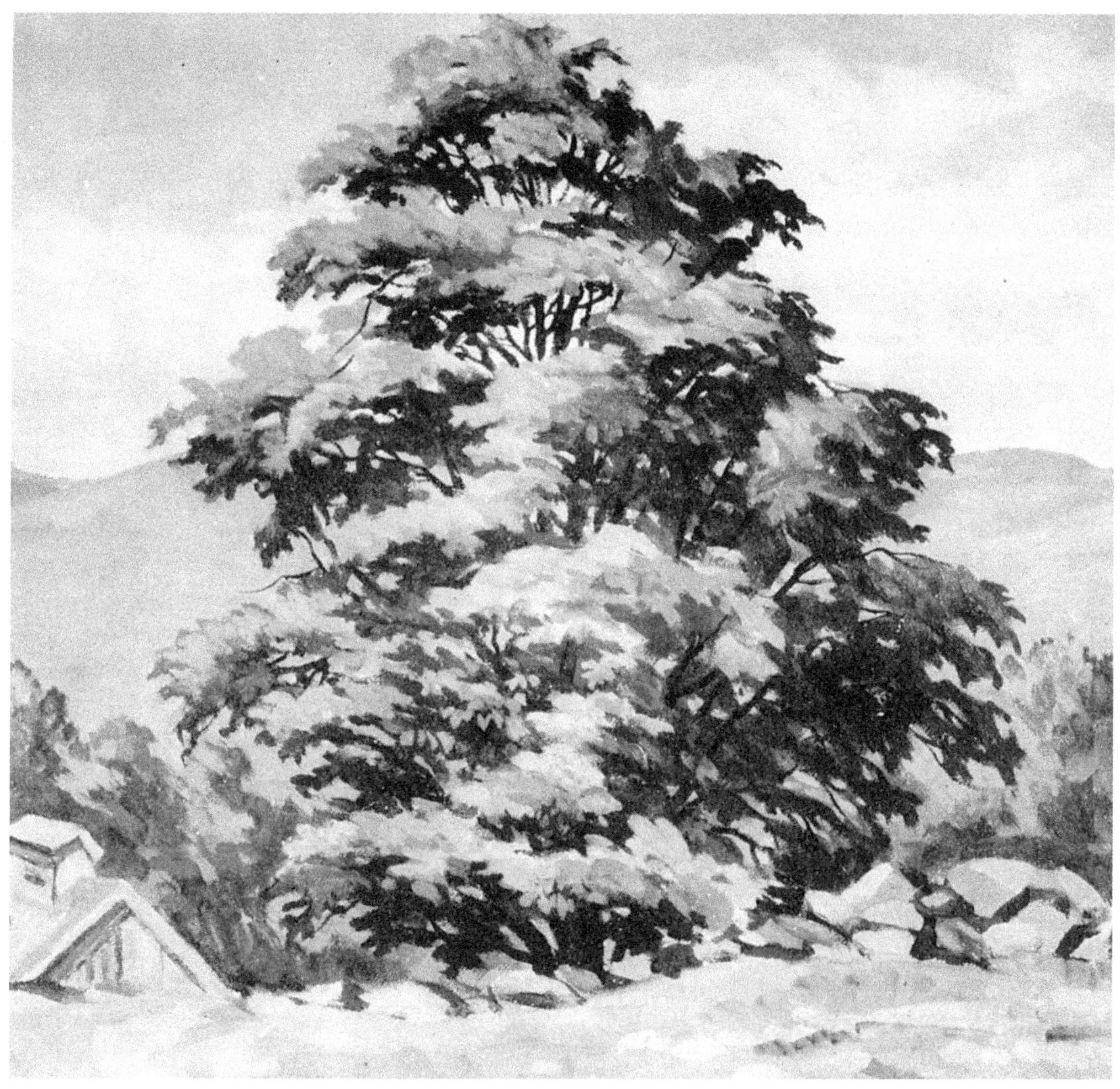

MAPLE. *Medium — Oil Paints on Canvas.* The difference between this tree and the maple on page 27 is due, perhaps, more to the different media employed than to the trees themselves. Both examples are typical — large masses of foliage, offering an excellent opportunity for showing light and shade, and a tendency toward a tapering or conical top. The greatest width, as a rule, is somewhat below the half height. Compare this with the elm silhouette. (See comment — page 22)

This picture, like the frontispiece and the one on page 60, were painted in full color and in translating the color values into terms of black and white, some values are bound to have changed somewhat. My reason for including them in this revised edition is to show that the same principles and feeling for design and structure are necessary regardless of the medium used and also to refute the statement, made by some painters, that you should "forget all you know about drawing when you take up color".

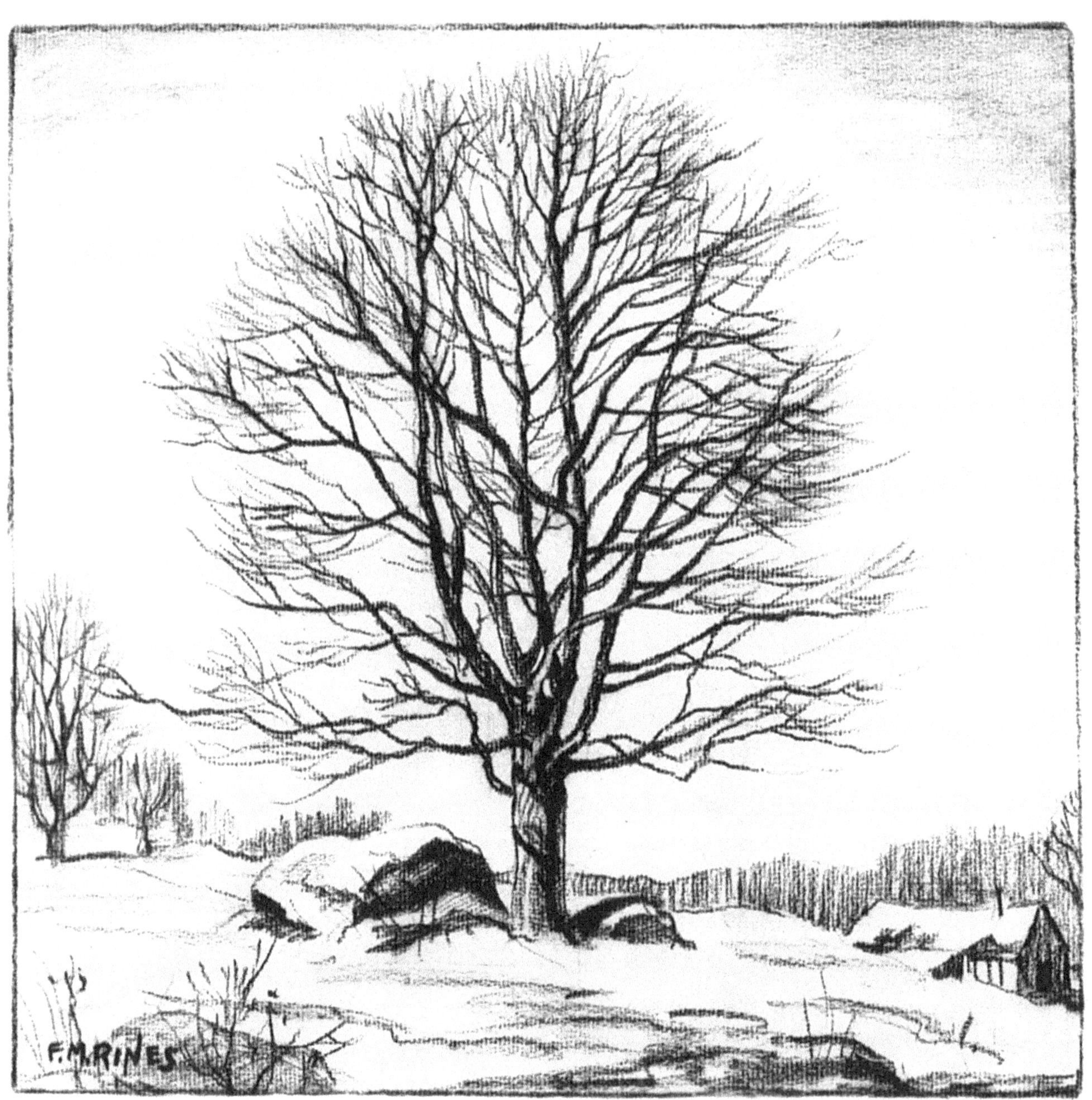

MAPLE. *Medium—Charcoal on White Charcoal Paper*. There are several different species of Maple — the one shown here and on the opposite page are Sugar Maples. The main trunk frequently extends to the height of the tree, unbroken by divisions, instead of as shown here — otherwise the character of the branch growth is the same. Most of the upper branches extend outward and upward, gradually changing to a more nearly horizontal direction nearer the base. The smaller twigs and branches are quite sturdy, and, while not as gnarled and tortuous as the oak, are not drooping or pendulous like the elm. This drawing and that of the birch in Winter have been reduced more than the other drawings because the charcoal, being a less delicate tool than the other media, it is easier to work on a somewhat larger scale.

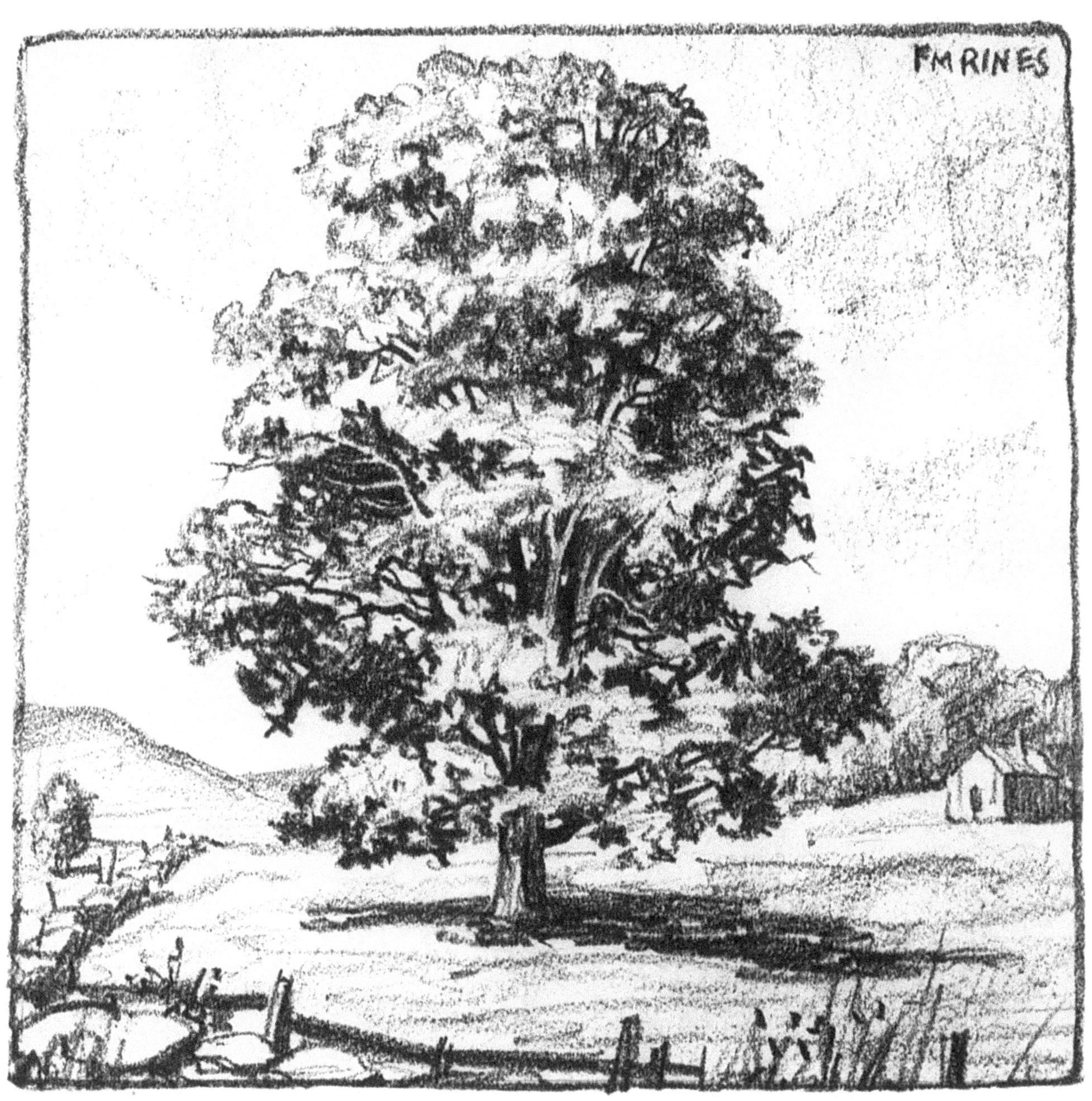

MAPLE. *Medium — Lithograph Crayon on Medium Surfaced Paper.* The leaves of the maple are large, and on healthy specimens, grow very thickly, hence the unusually good opportunity to bring out large, sharply contrasting masses of sunlight and the consequent shadow areas. The silhouette is often very symmetrical, sometimes too much so for pictorial interest; therefore, do not hesitate to break up the contour a bit if necessary, without, of course deviating too much from its characteristic form. Notice how, in spite of the thick foliage, the structure, as shown on the opposite page, is still evident through the leaves. Compare the scale of strokes in this drawing with those of the locust in Summer on page 33. This is an extremely important factor.

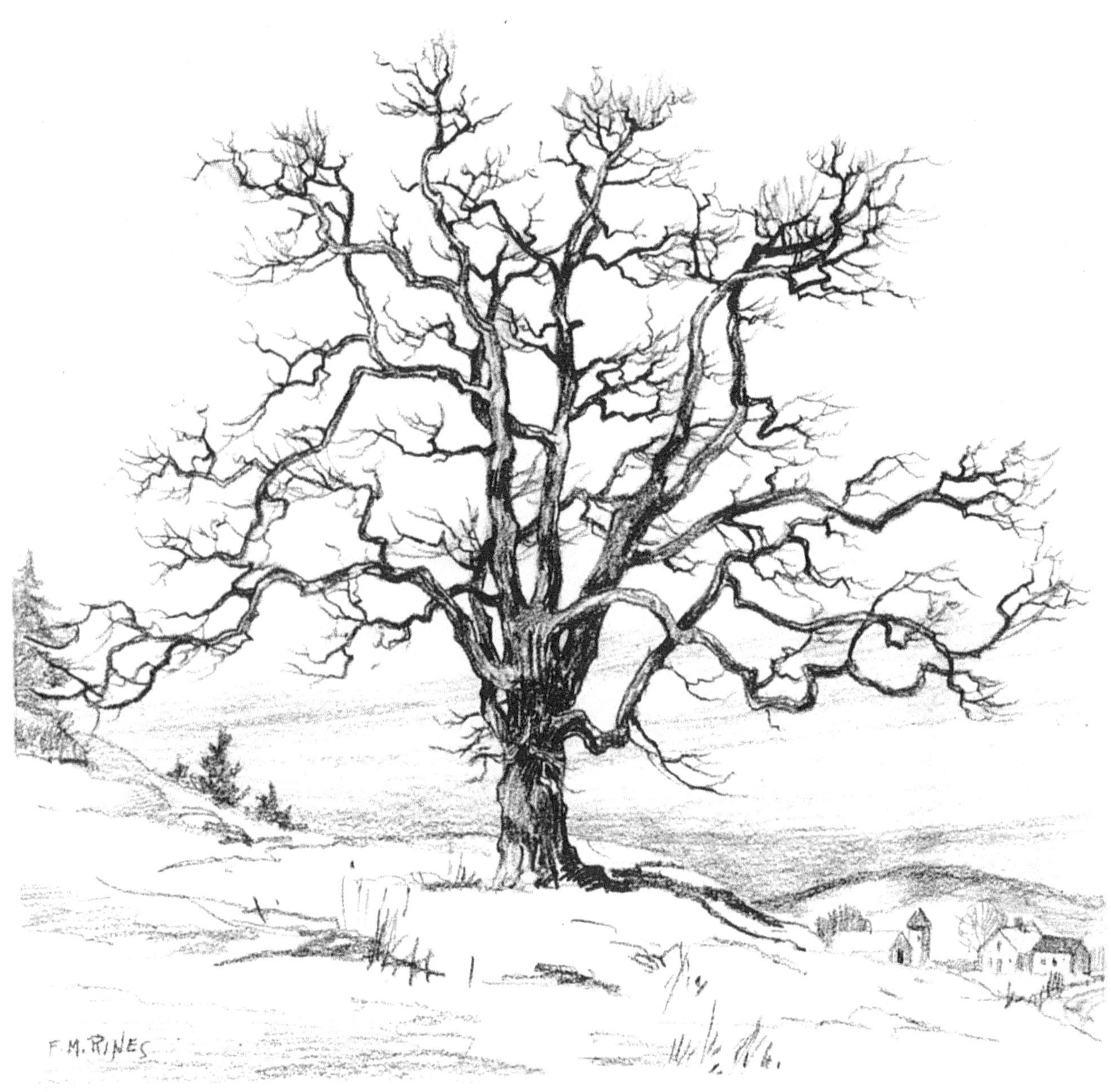

WHITE OAK. *Medium — Carbon Crayon on Medium Surfaced Stock*. The sturdiness or ruggedness of the oak is one of its outstanding characteristics. When growing in the open, as they very frequently do, it is a wide spreading tree, with the lower branches extending almost horizontally for a considerable distance, and often, as in the one illustrated (an old, considerably weather-beaten specimen), angular and tortuous. The twigs, also, while inclined to be rather short, are very angular, and reach in all directions. The main trunk often extends the length of the tree, instead of dividing, as this one does. When sheltered by surrounding growth the dead, brown leaves often remain on the tree throughout the Winter.

[28]

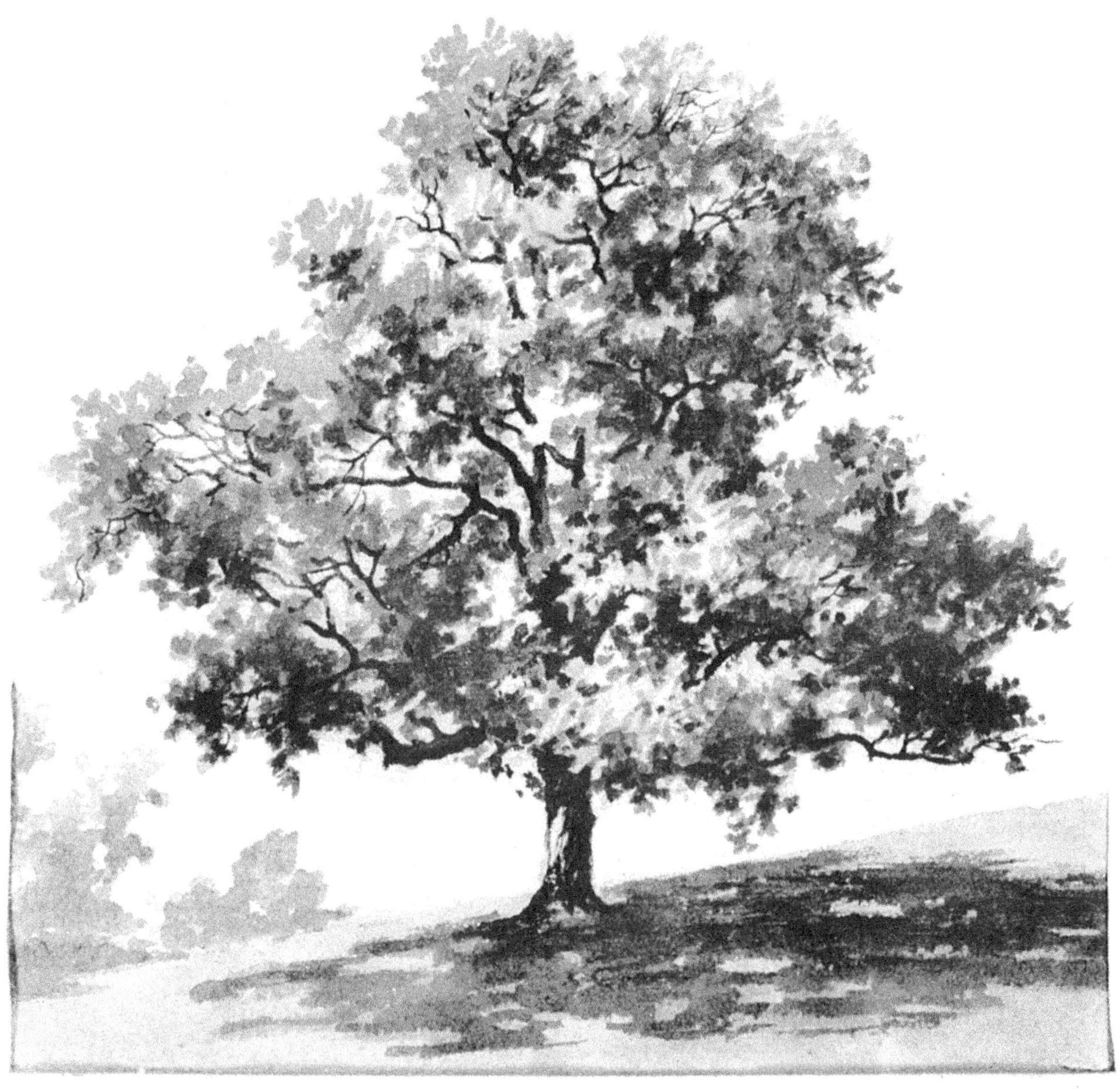

WHITE OAK. *Medium — Burnt Sienna Water Color Wash, on Water Color Paper.*
Some of the characteristics of the oak, as described on the opposite page, are not so evident in
Summer, due to its large, thickly massed leaves; nevertheless, they are sufficiently so to make
it easily distinguishable. Due to the fact that the foliage is of a rather dark color, the light masses
are not so conspicuous as in some other trees. In the drawing, however, they can be forced a
bit. The tree pictured here is a somewhat more perfect specimen than the one in Winter; it is
younger, and has not suffered so much from the ravages of the storms.

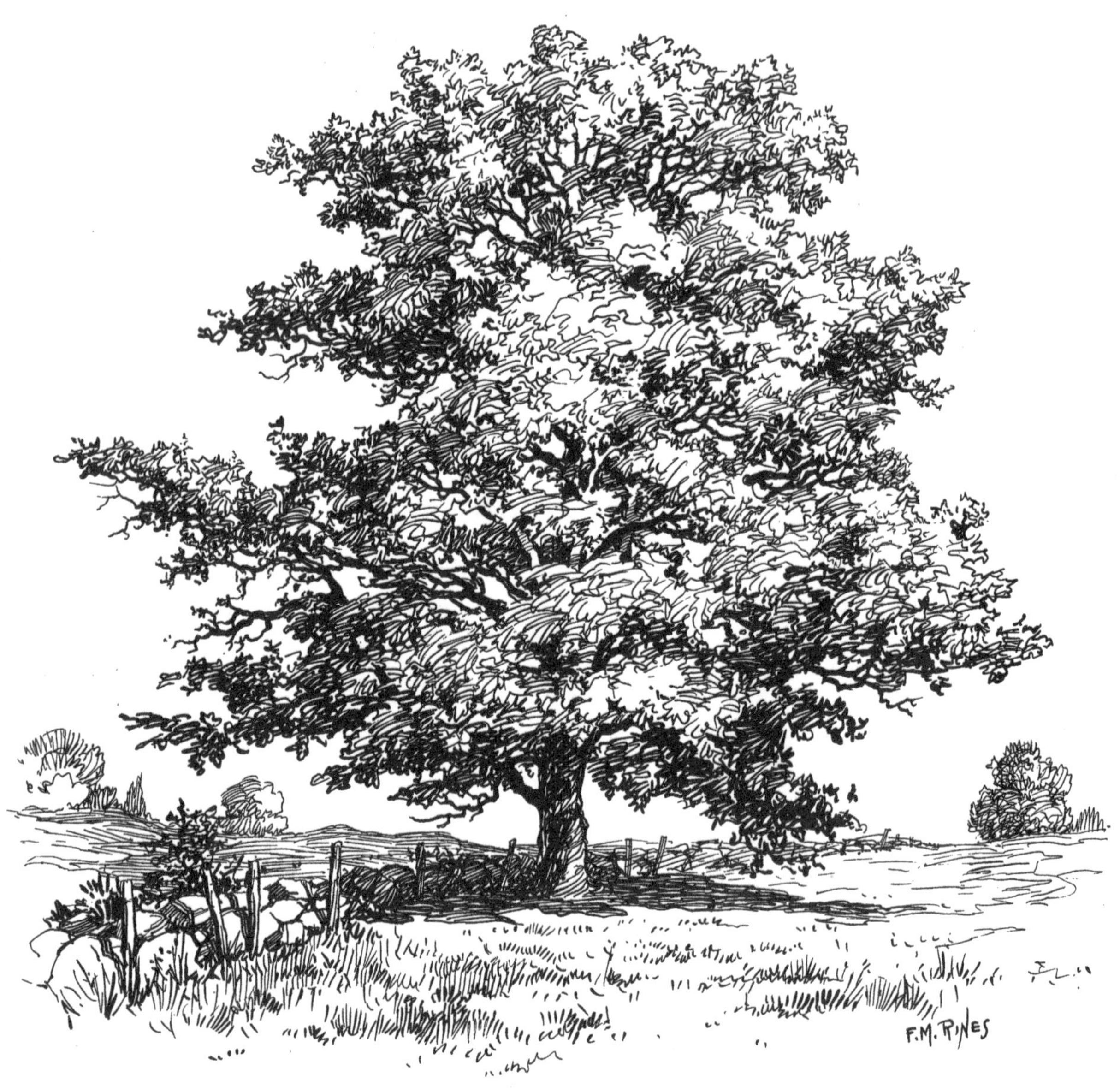

WHITE OAK. *Medium—Pen and Ink on Smooth Paper.* While the general character of this oak is not much different from the one on the preceding page, it is introduced to illustrate the contrast between the techniques of the two media. The direction of the leaf growth as suggested by the brush strokes in the wash drawing are emphasized much more by the pen strokes in this illustration. Also, the light foliage masses, when rendered in wash, are toned slightly, while in the pen drawing they are represented by the pure white paper, broken up just sufficiently to distinguish them from the sky spaces.

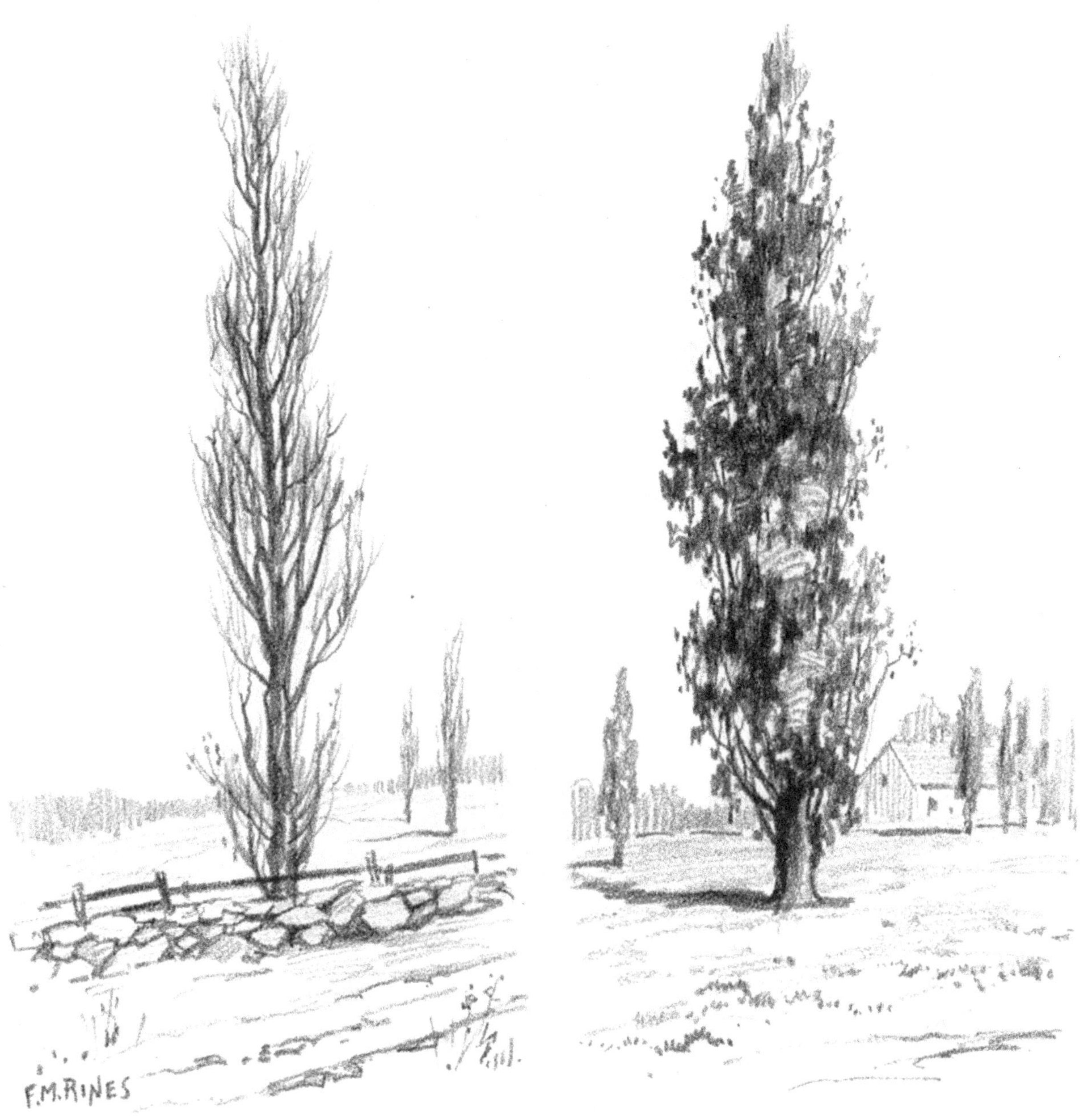

LOMBARDY POPLAR. *Medium—Carbon Crayon on Medium Rough Paper.* This tree is a native of Italy, but has been planted so much in this country, especially around dwellings and along village streets, that it seems advisable to include it in this series. When growing by itself (instead of in rows, for screens and windbreaks) it has considerable character. Its most notable feature is the distinct upward trend of its branches. It usually has one straight trunk, extending through to the top, but sometimes this trunk divides part way up into two or three smaller ones. When brought in to a composition containing a mass of rounded foliage, the effect is often quite pleasing — the question of contrast again.

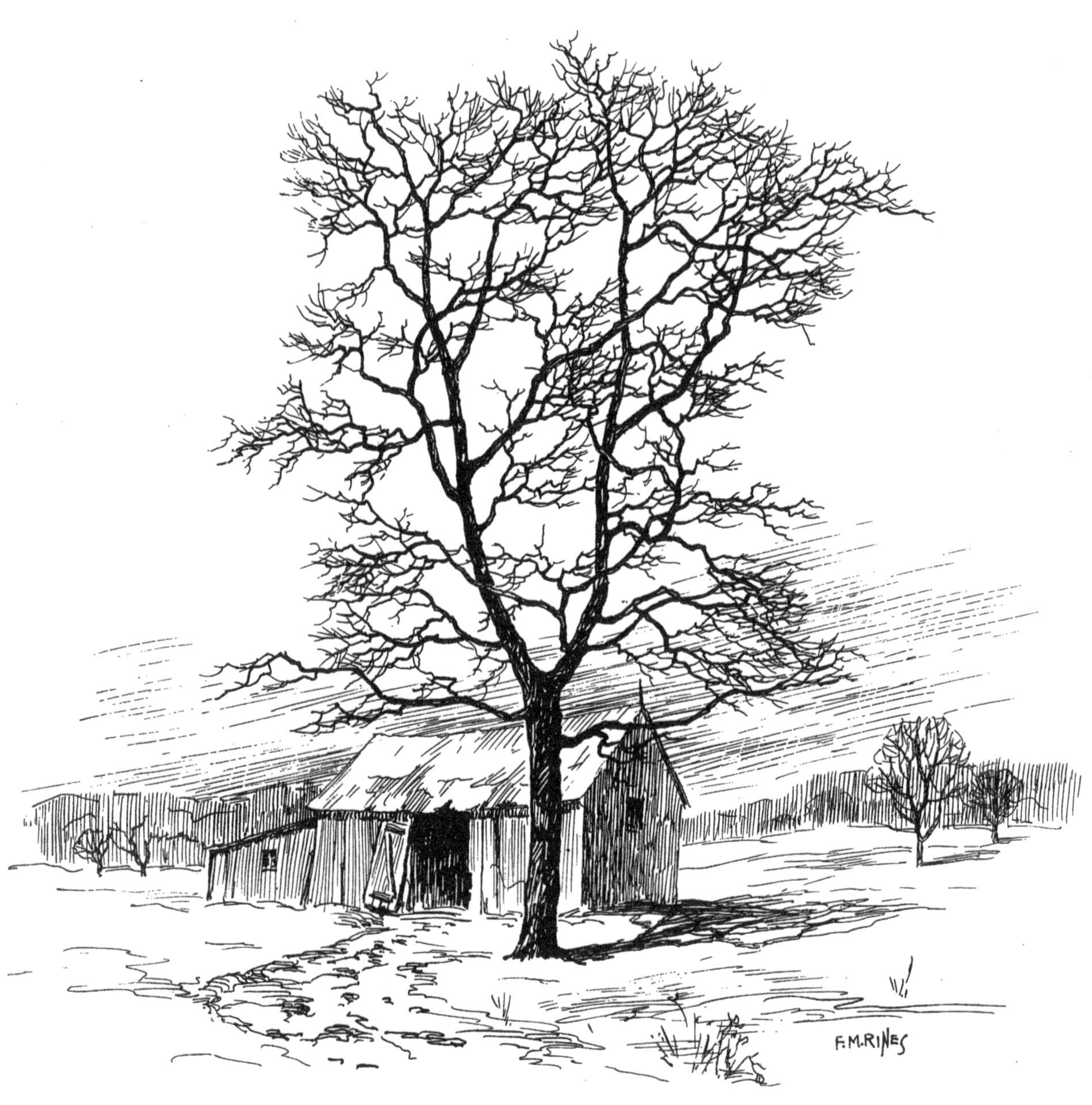

COMMON LOCUST. *Medium—Pen and Ink*. The locust is a fairly tall tree, with twisted and angular twigs and branches. In the northern part of the country it does not leaf out until so much later, and sheds its foliage so much earlier than other trees, that it often appears to be dead. Advantage of this fact can sometimes be taken to afford an interesting contrast to a mass of trees in full leaf. The trunk usually divides, at a height of fifteen or twenty feet, into two or three large branches. The Honey Locust is very similar to the Common Locust in general growth except that it often grows much larger and has a number of spikey thorns, giving it an even more ragged, or scraggly, appearance.

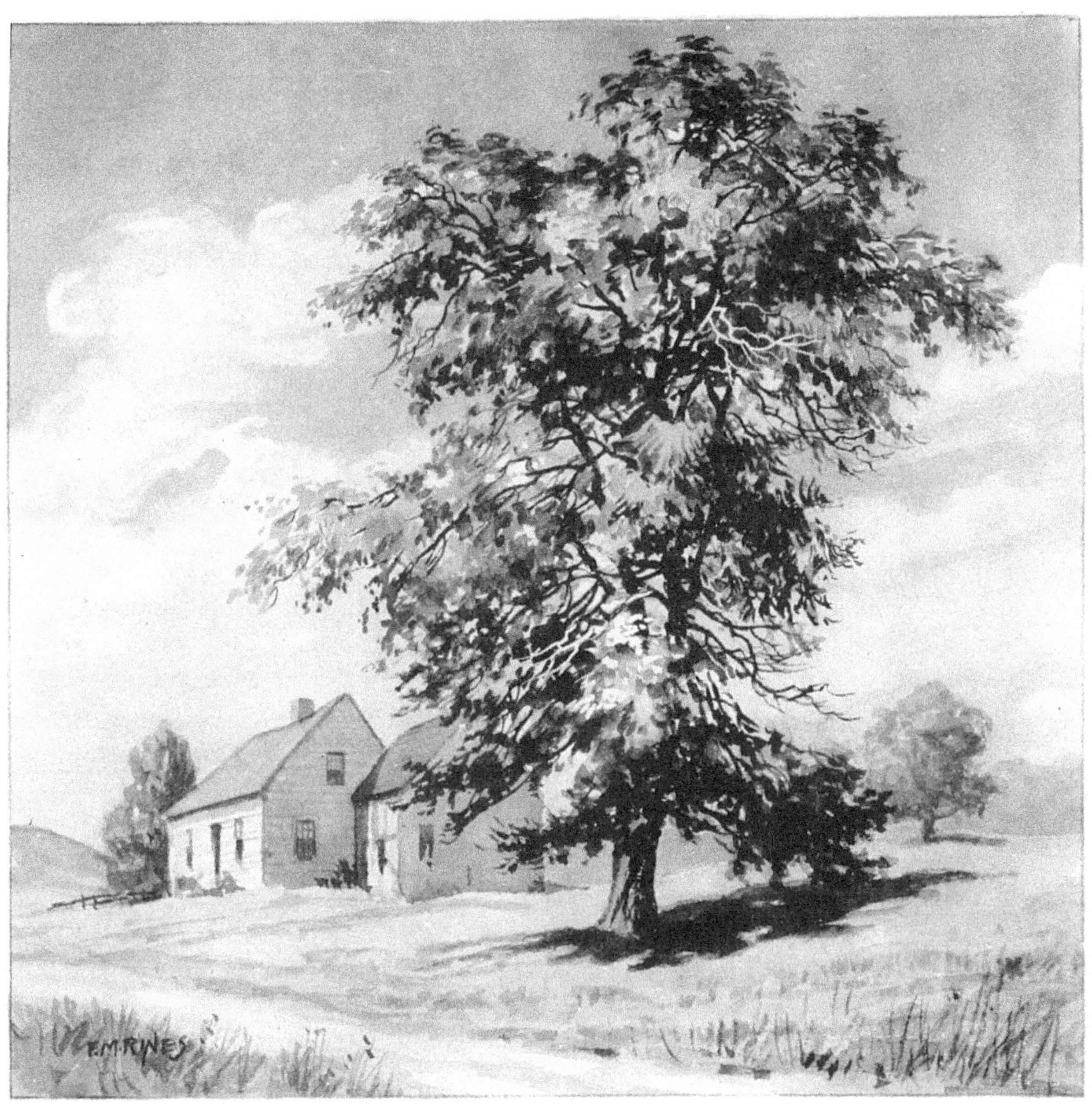

LOCUST. *Medium—Charcoal Gray Water Color Wash.* Although the locust has very fine leaves, they are so thickly massed that there is no difficulty in distinguishing the sunlight and shadows areas. It is on the silhouetted edges that this fine leafy texture should be most in evidence, although, of course, the different masses of foliage are also affected to a certain extent. Compare the manner in which the technique of this drawing and of the maple, for instance, bring out this difference in leaf scale. The strokes of the brush are applied in the same manner as would be pencil strokes — the only way in which the character of the tree can be indicated.

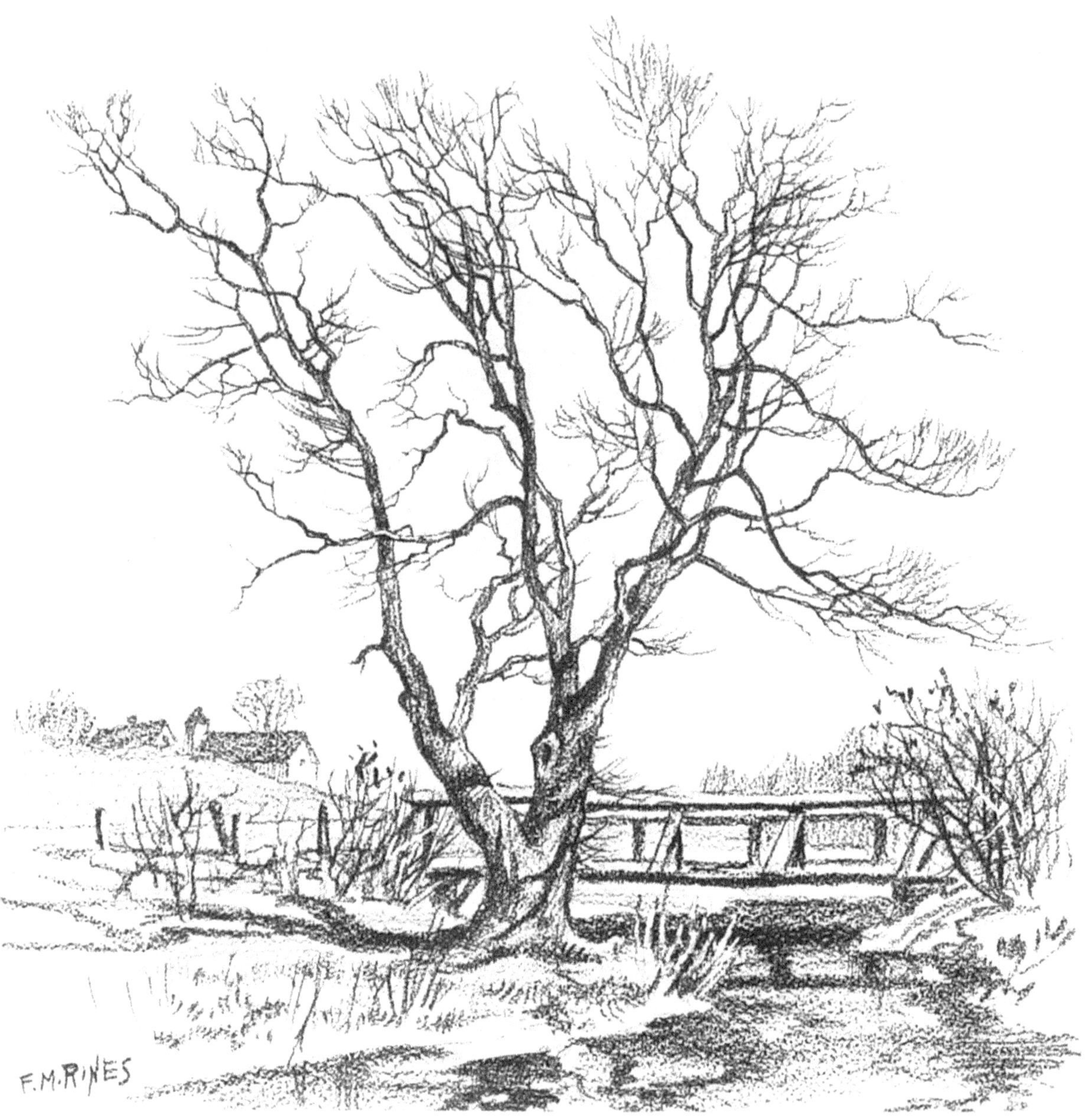

WILLOW. *Medium—Carbon Crayon, on rough surface.* The willows vary greatly in structure. Since the wood is brittle, storms often break large branches. These branches, unless entirely separated from the tree, continue to grow. As a result, the appearance of the willow changes a great deal from year to year. The tendency of the twigs is to grow upward from the larger branches. These larger branches grow in all directions; some grow almost horizontally from the main trunks, and are often gnarled and distorted. Willows usually grow in low land where there is more or less moisture, and along the banks of streams. While not a graceful tree, the willow is almost always picturesque, and, therefore, fits admirably into compositions.

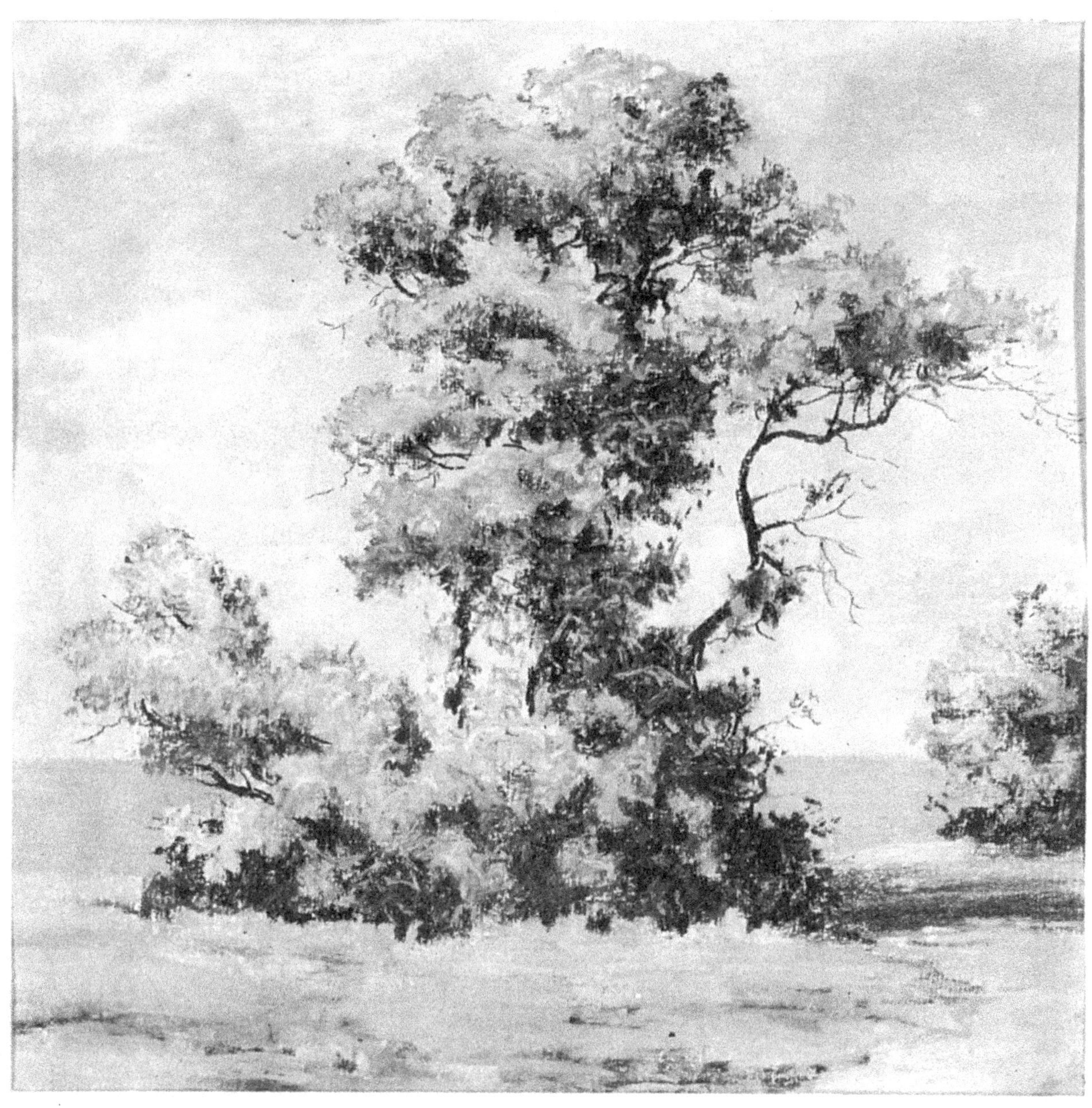

WILLOW. *Medium — Pastel*. The individual leaves of the willow are quite small, but grow so thickly that the light and shade masses are very evident. Willow foliage, as a rule, presents great variety, growing very thickly on some parts, and more sparsely in others. In these sparser areas, especially in old trees, many small twigs are in evidence. A number of these twigs may be dead. Introducing some of these in the drawing adds greatly to the picturesque effect previously mentioned. The local color of willow foliage is quite light; consequently the dark trunks appear darker in comparison giving the tree a "snappy" or contrasting appearance. The delicacy of willow foliage in early Spring offers an exceptionally fine opportunity for color work.

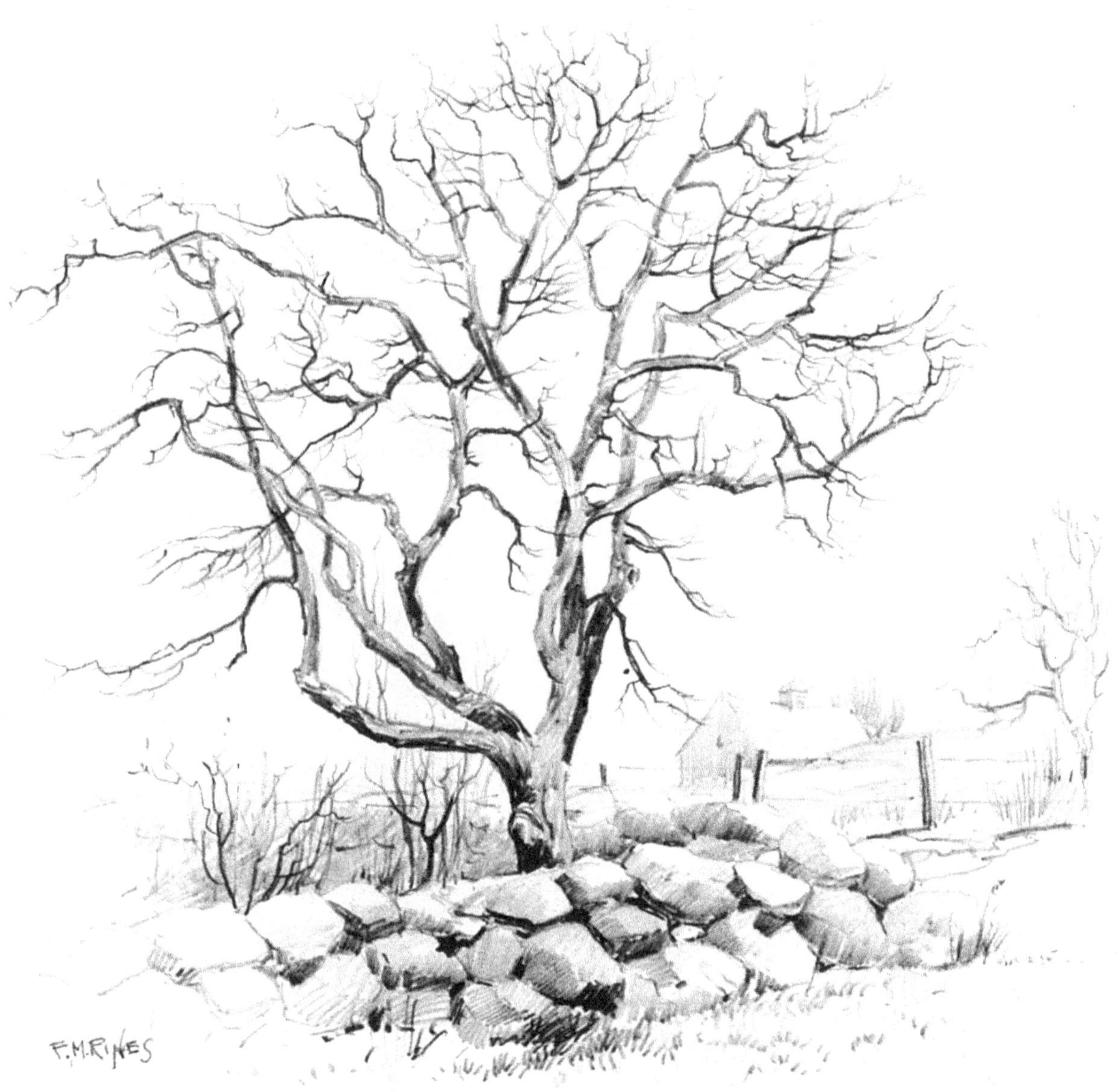

APPLE. *Medium—Pencil*. No tree varies more in general form and no tree, when allowed to grow naturally, is more interesting or picturesque, than the apple tree. Some of its outstanding features are its twisted, oftentimes writhing limbs and its angular twigs. Contrasting with these, on old trees are frequent straight shoots, or "suckers" as they are called. On well-trimmed trees these latter are cut off, as they sap the life of the tree. Due to the weight of the fruit in Summer, most apple trees show traces of where some limbs have been broken off. In the Spring, there is no more beautiful sight than an apple tree in full blossom. It is next to impossible, however, to attempt to produce this effect in black and white. Color alone can do it justice.

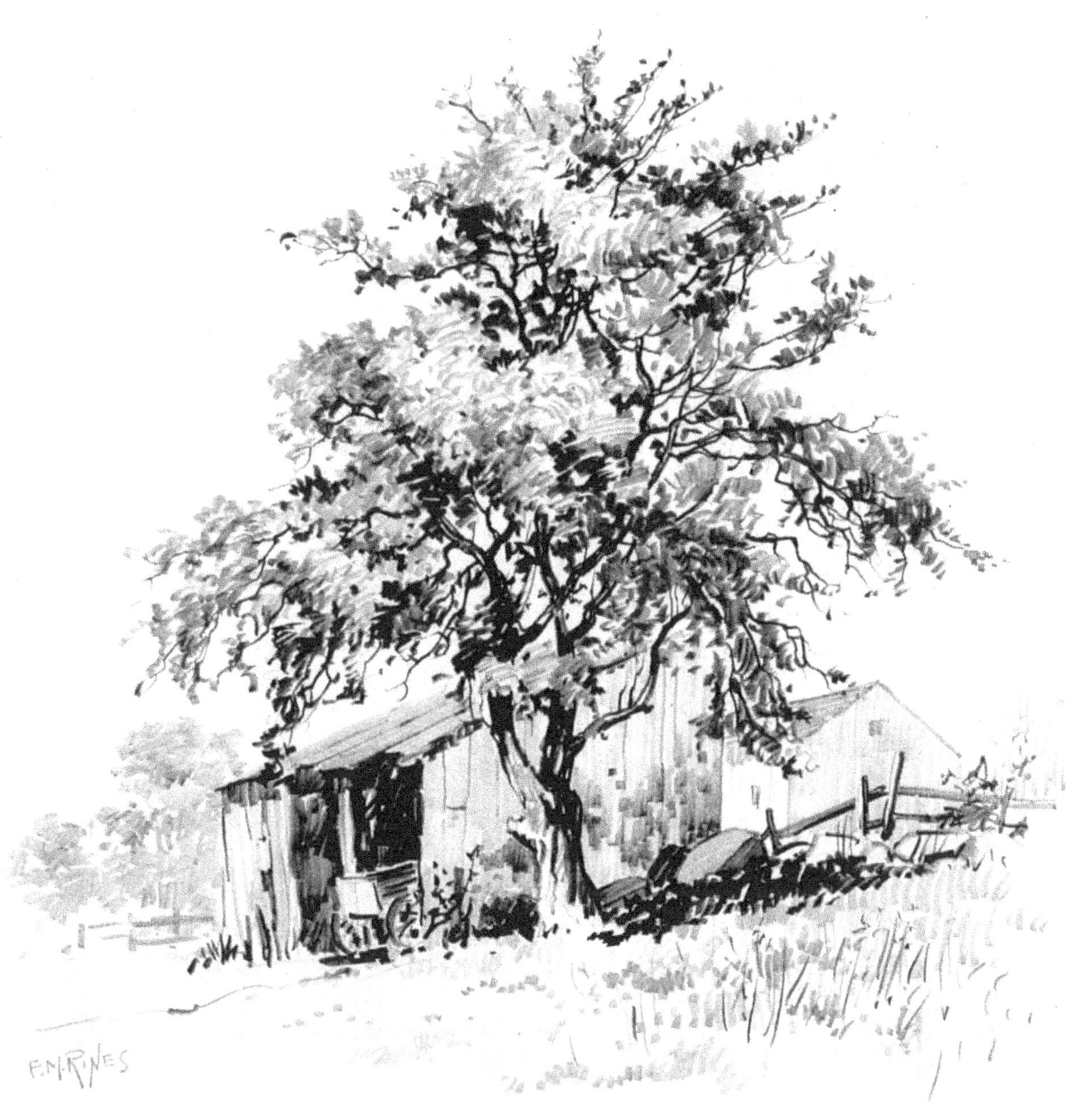

APPLE. *Medium—Pencil.* The entirely different forms of the apple tree on this and the preceding page are only two of thousands that these interesting trees assume. One feature of apple tree foliage that makes it distinct from that of other species is the straight, new shoots sticking out at all angles from the general massing. While these are especially evident at the top of the tree, they occur more or less around the edge. While usually not as thickly foliaged as some other trees, the leaves grow quite massed on some branches, consequently giving an opportunity to show much of the construction, or anatomy, in some spots, as well as sunlit masses in other places. Compare the absence of symmetrical silhouette of these trees with the opposite extreme of the maple.

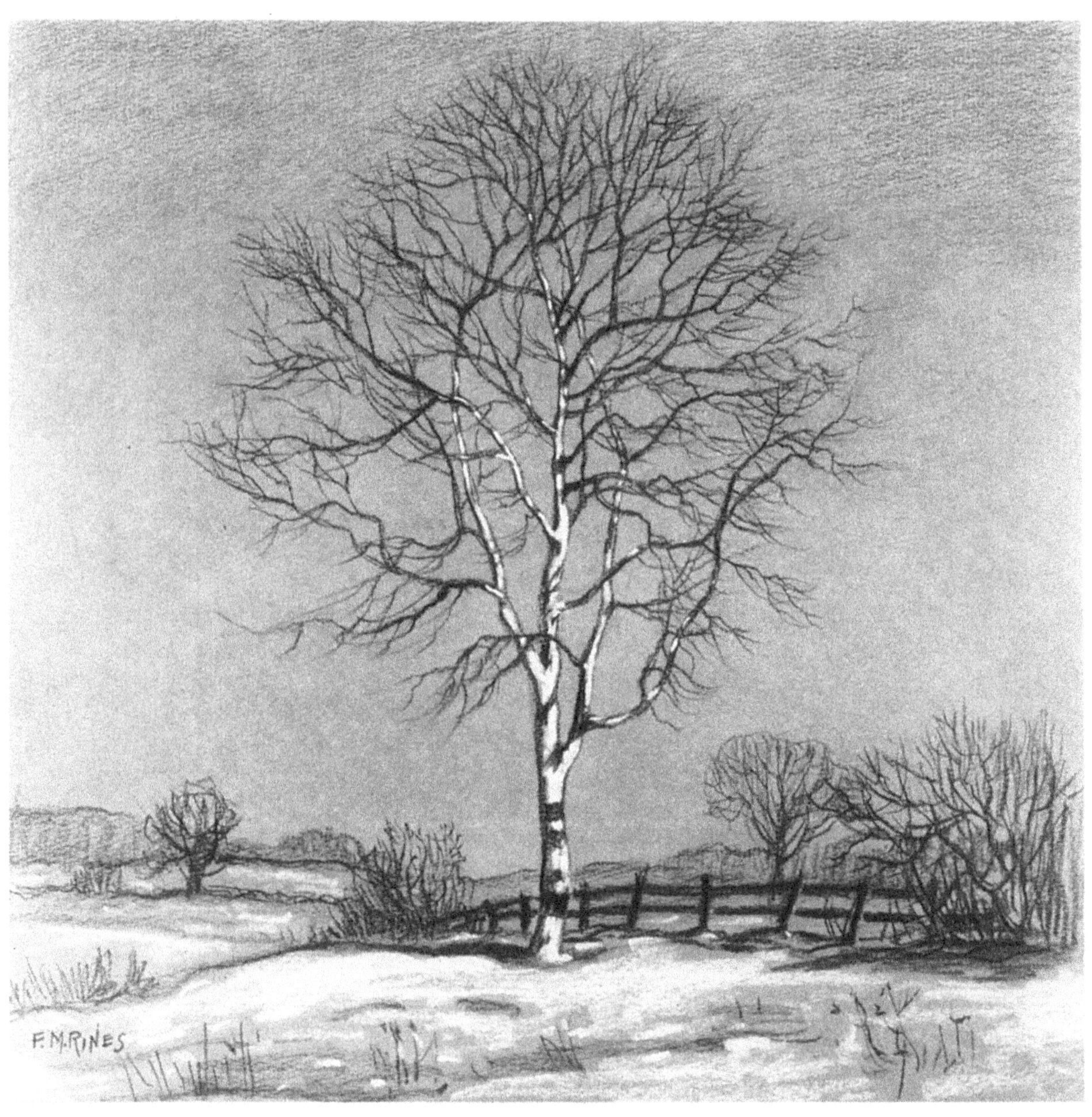

BIRCH. *Medium—Charcoal and White Chalk on Toned Charcoal Paper.* While not a large tree as a rule (it seldom exceeds thirty or forty feet in height) the birch is always a conspicuous note in any landscape. This is due largely to its snow white bark on the main trunk, in sharp contrast to almost any background. The smaller limbs and twigs are quite slender and graceful, and are dark brown, sometimes almost black in color, forming a dark triangular shaped spot where they branch out from the trunk. The dark patches where the white trunk has been girdled, so frequently seen, affords a further pleasing contrast. The birch is an extremely hardy tree, often being found farther north than any other deciduous tree.

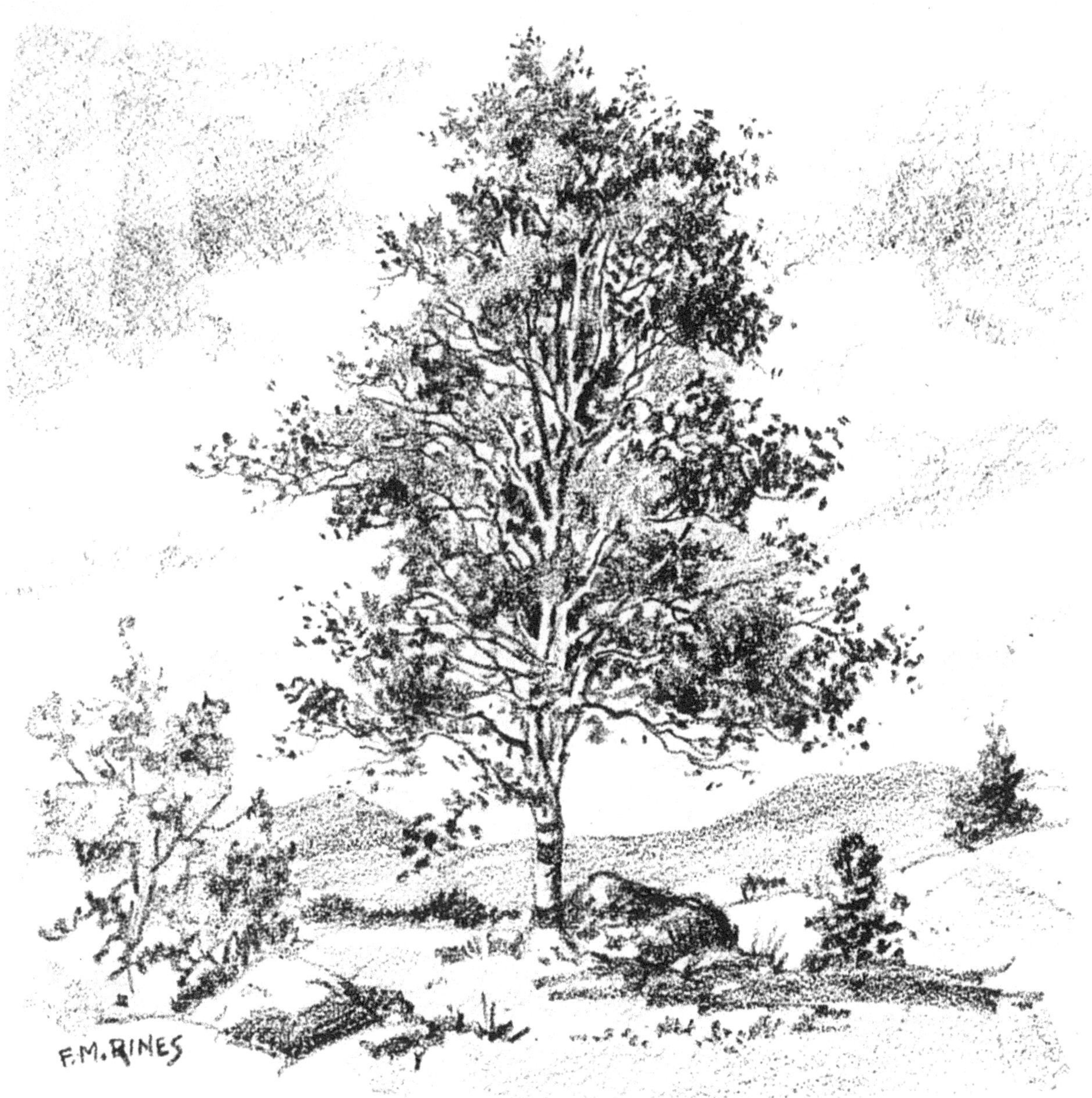

BIRCH *Medium—Lithograph Crayon on Water Color Paper*. The leaves of the birch
tree are rather small and in many instances do not grow as thickly as some of the other trees.
For these reasons it does not offer the opportunity for such distinct light and dark masses as does,
for instance, the maple, the willow or the elm. The general appearance is therefore inclined to
be flatter than these other trees. The contrast of the white bark on the trunk and the dark green
of the foliage lends itself very nicely to semi-decorative effects in paintings. For the most part,
when growing wild, birches appear in groups of from two to eight or ten, and when near a pond
or stream lean out over the water.

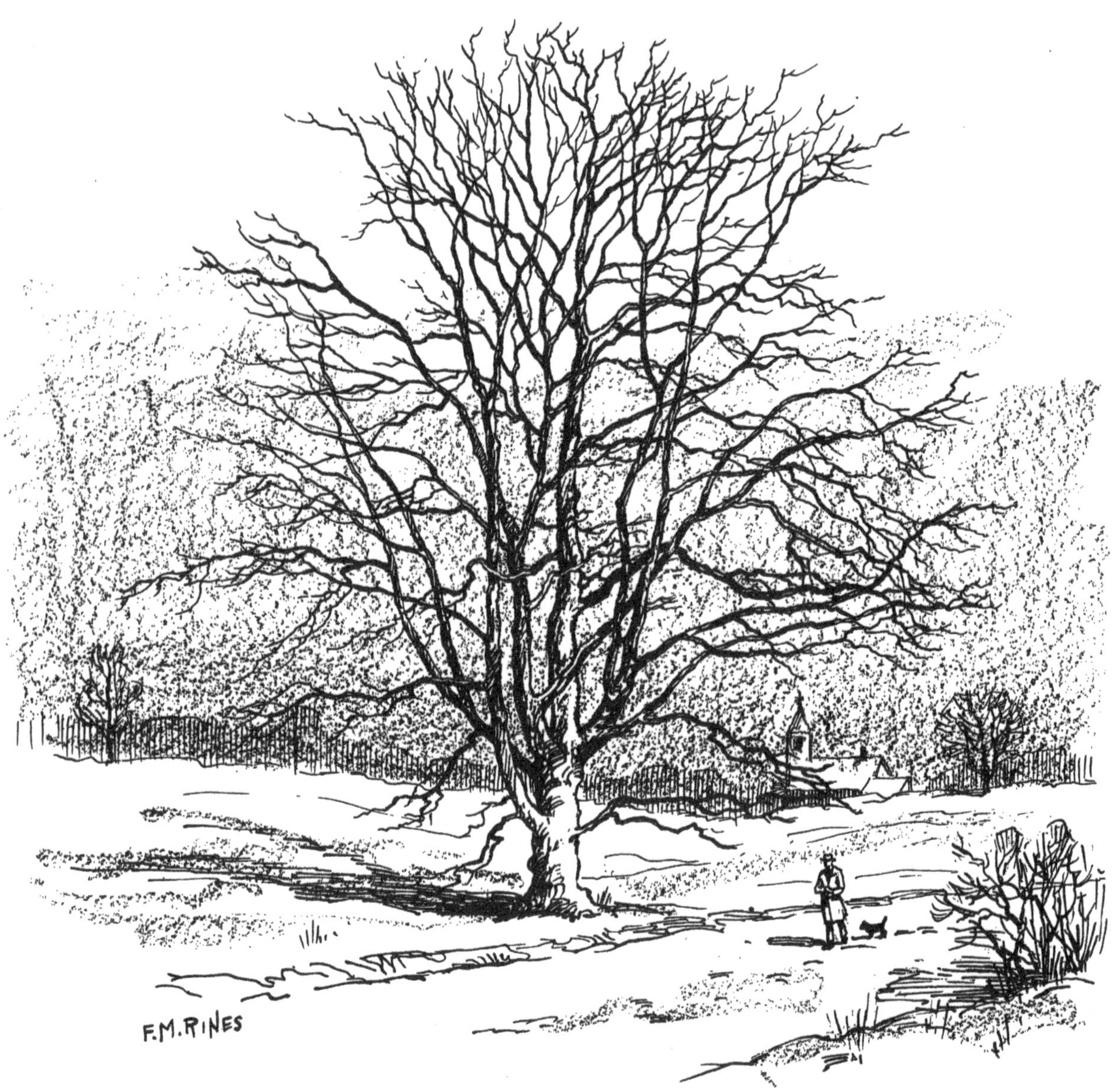

BEECH. *Medium—Pen and Ink with a touch or two of Lithograph Crayon in sky, etc.*
The beech tree, like the oak, maple, and many other trees, often has the main trunk more emphasized than the one in this picture, especially when closely grouped with other trees. One of its outstanding characteristics is its smooth silvery gray bark—a difficult effect to produce with black and white, but easily shown with color. Horizontal branches often grow very near the ground. Belonging to the same family as the oaks, it often assumes many of the oaks' peculiarities of growth. Its very evident light trunk and branch coloring, however, serve to make it always readily distinguishable. Although a native forest tree, it is frequently found in parks and gardens.

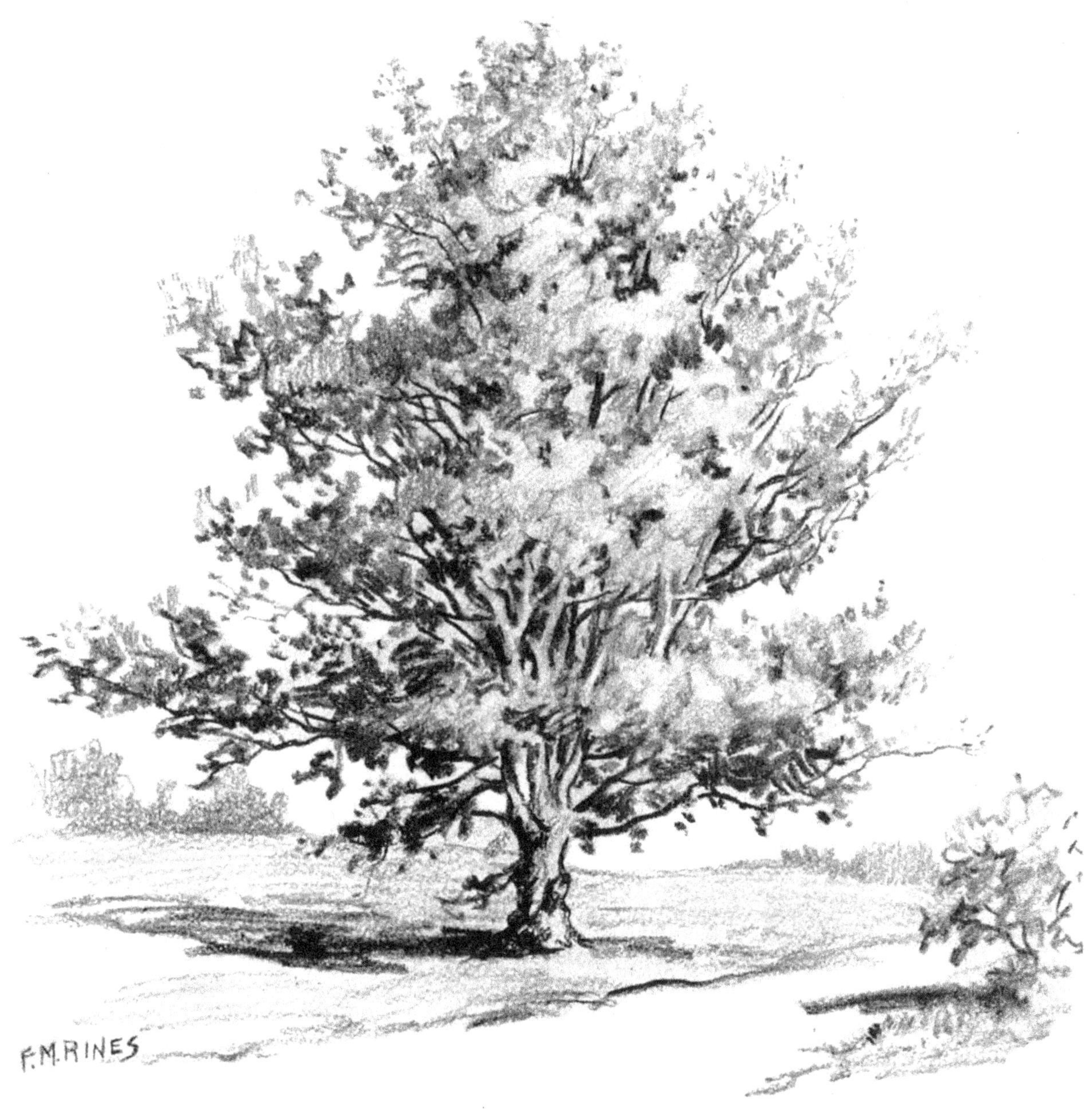

BEECH. *Medium—Charcoal on Rough Surfaced Paper.* The top part of this beech is much more pointed than the one shown in Winter. Both of these forms are equally typical. The foliage of beeches is a delicate green in the Spring time and yellow in the Fall, and combined with the bark color, already described, makes it an extremely interesting tree for painters, especially when growing along with other trees, more usual in coloring.

This rendering was smooched a little in the light areas and the highlights were then picked out with the kneaded eraser. Some of the light branches were produced in the same manner.

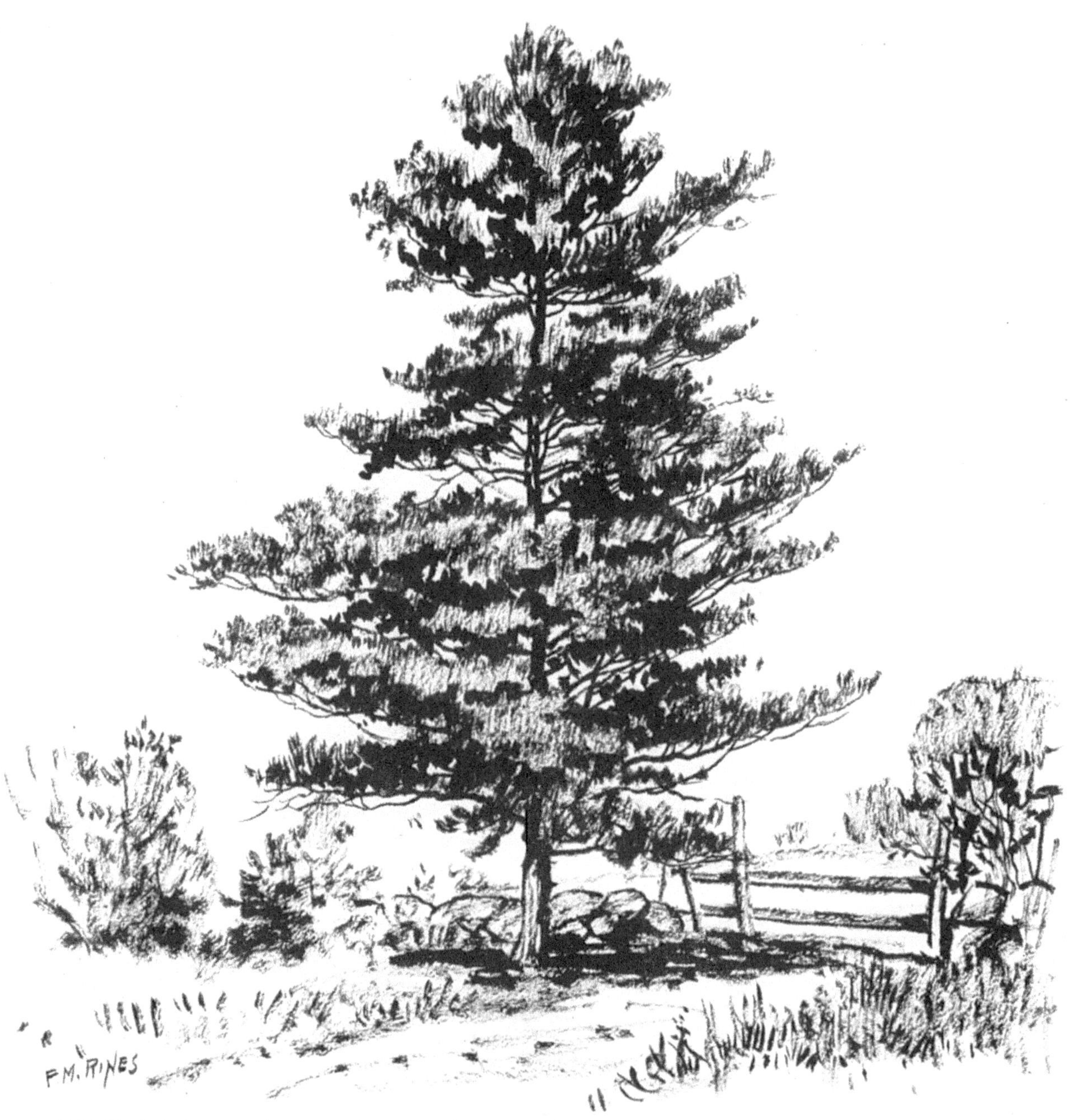

PINE. *Medium—Dry Brush and Ink*. One of our most widely distributed as well as most beautiful trees, its dark green foliage makes its an equally outstanding note in either a Winter or a Summer landscape. A particularly conspicuous feature is its almost horizontal branching, with their upward growing twigs from which the "needles," or foliage, grow. Like the other trees, the newest growth, at the top, extends almost vertically. The heavy foliage on some limbs and the scanty growth on others, exposing the twigs and branches, tends to give a great deal of character to this tree, in addition to its silhouette. Notice that there is little or none of the curving strokes, so evident in the drawings of other trees; the strokes suggest more stiffness, and are all more or less vertical.

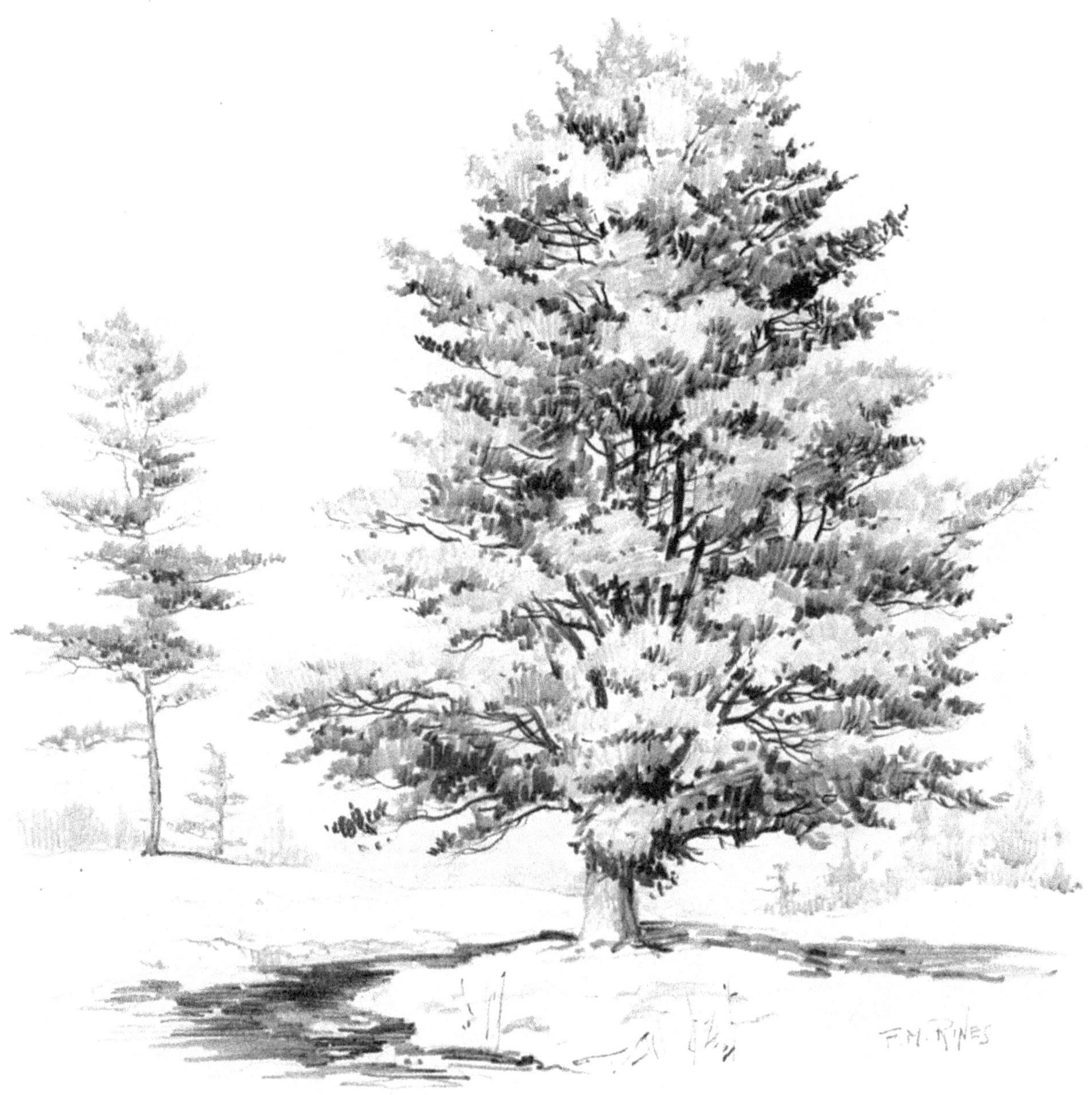

PINE. *Medium—Pencil.* This pine tree is a less familiar, but no less characteristic one, than that shown opposite. It is what is commonly termed a "pasture pine" — that is, it has grown entirely in the open, away from other trees. Consequently, the single stem so evident in the other drawing, has in this case divided into several heavy limbs with an accompanying upward growth of branches. Eventually the same horizontal branches appear, however. The same vertical direction for both the pencil and the brush strokes is used, because they are so strongly noticeable in the actual foliage. The chief difference in the growth of the pine tree in comparison with most other conifers, is that on the pine the twigs grow upward from the branches, instead of down ward as they do on the others; also the branches themselves, on the spruce, hemlock, etc., have a tendency to droop.

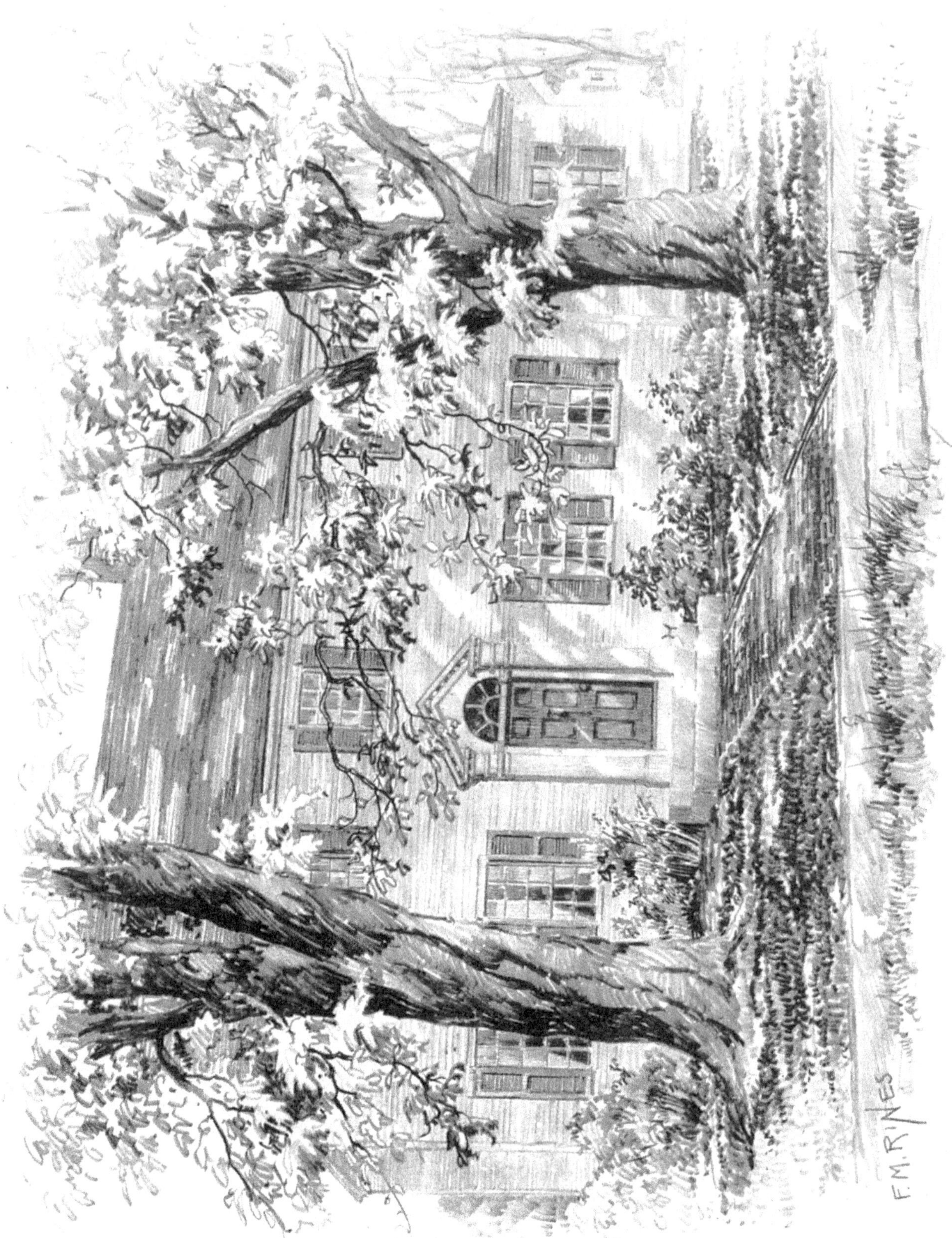

SUNLIGHT AND SHADOW

Medium—Pencil. These two big trees are horse chestnuts, which have unusually large leaves. One of the most difficult problems in drawing trees is to show them against some background other than sky. Painting them in oils or pastels is much easier because the oils or the pastels, being opaque, can be superimposed over the background. In pencil, however, the design of the foliage must be exceptionally carefully drawn. Then the background must be rendered, leaving the foliage as white paper until this background is complete. The edge of the foliage silhouette must then be rendered, working from the background into the tree masses, breaking them up as much or as little as is necessary to bring out sufficient contrast.

By keeping the front of the house mostly in shadow and taking advantage of the aforementioned large leaves, which grow in clumps, is one way of solving this difficulty. Another way would be to reverse the arrangement of light and dark, i.e.— have the front of the house in brilliant sunlight and the leaves in dark silhouette against light.

The gnarled trunk of the tree on the left is very characteristic of the horse chestnut and affords a nice contrast with the texture of the house. Notice the difference in the branching of the two trunks. Both ways are typical.

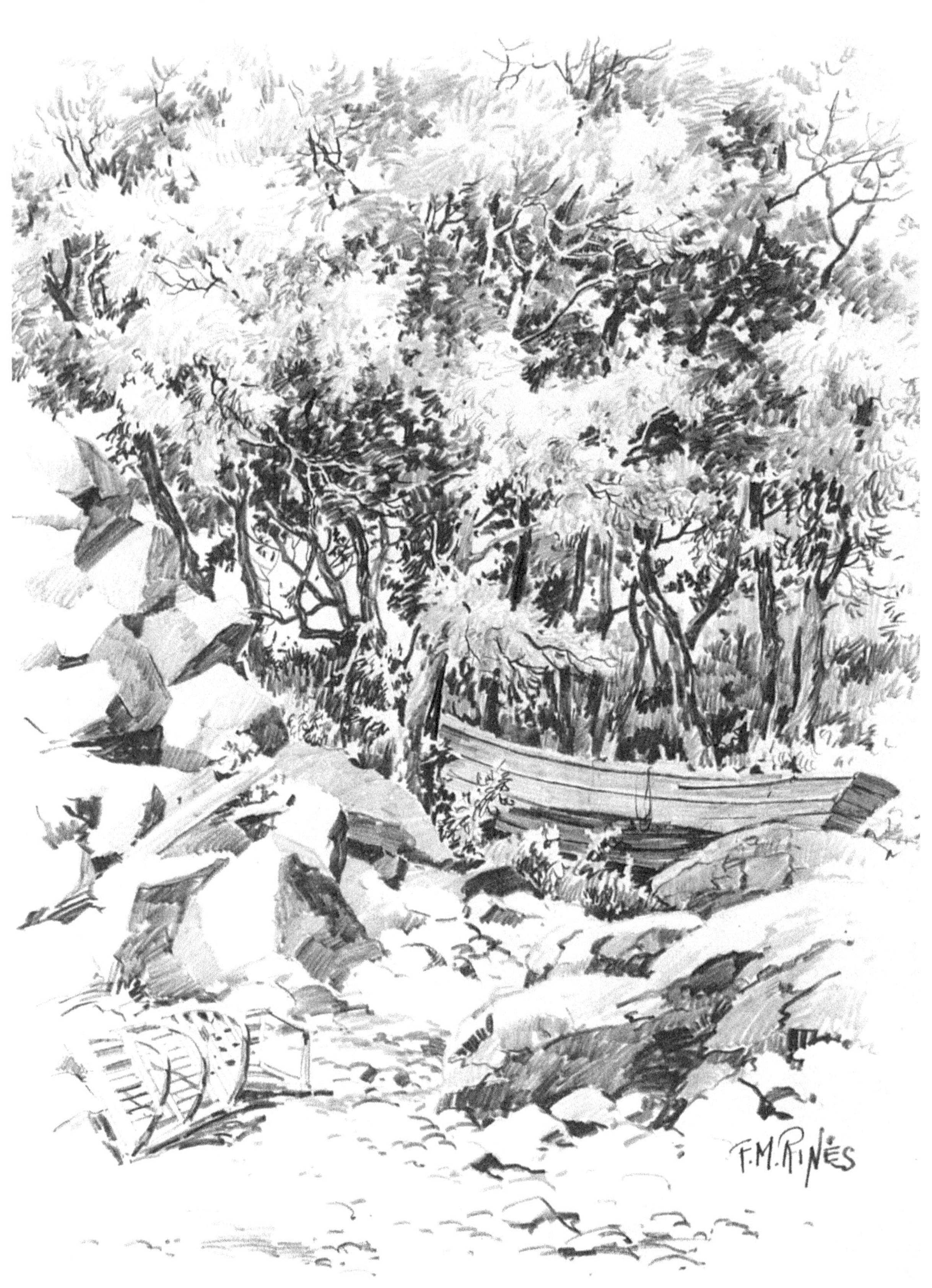

ROCKS AND WILLOWS

Medium—Pencil. This sketch depicts a group of willows growing so closely together that they constitute a miniature jungle. Each
individual tree so lost its identity that the effect is not of a silhouette,
but rather, a jumble of light and dark masses of foliage, interspersed
with twigs, branches and trunks. To select a few of these foliage
masses and to rearrange and compose them pleasingly is the problem
confronting the artist, when faced with similar scenes. While at first
glance, perhaps, the foliage, as represented here may seem to have
little in common with that of the "portrait" of the willow, a closer
inspection will reveal the same characteristic, fine leafy texture, the
same gnarled and distorted branches and the same open and heavily
massed areas.

The suggestion of sky, with the silhouetted trunks against it,
which appeared in the actual view, was used to advantage in the
sketch "*not* just because it *was* that way" but because it forms a wel-
come note of contrast to so much heavy massing of foliage above it.
Observe the introduction of a bit of detail here and there, also
for the sake of relief, from the broader *suggested* portions.

The large, simply treated rocks, further contrast the comparatively "busy" foliage areas, and the old boat and lobster trap add a
touch of human interest to the scene.

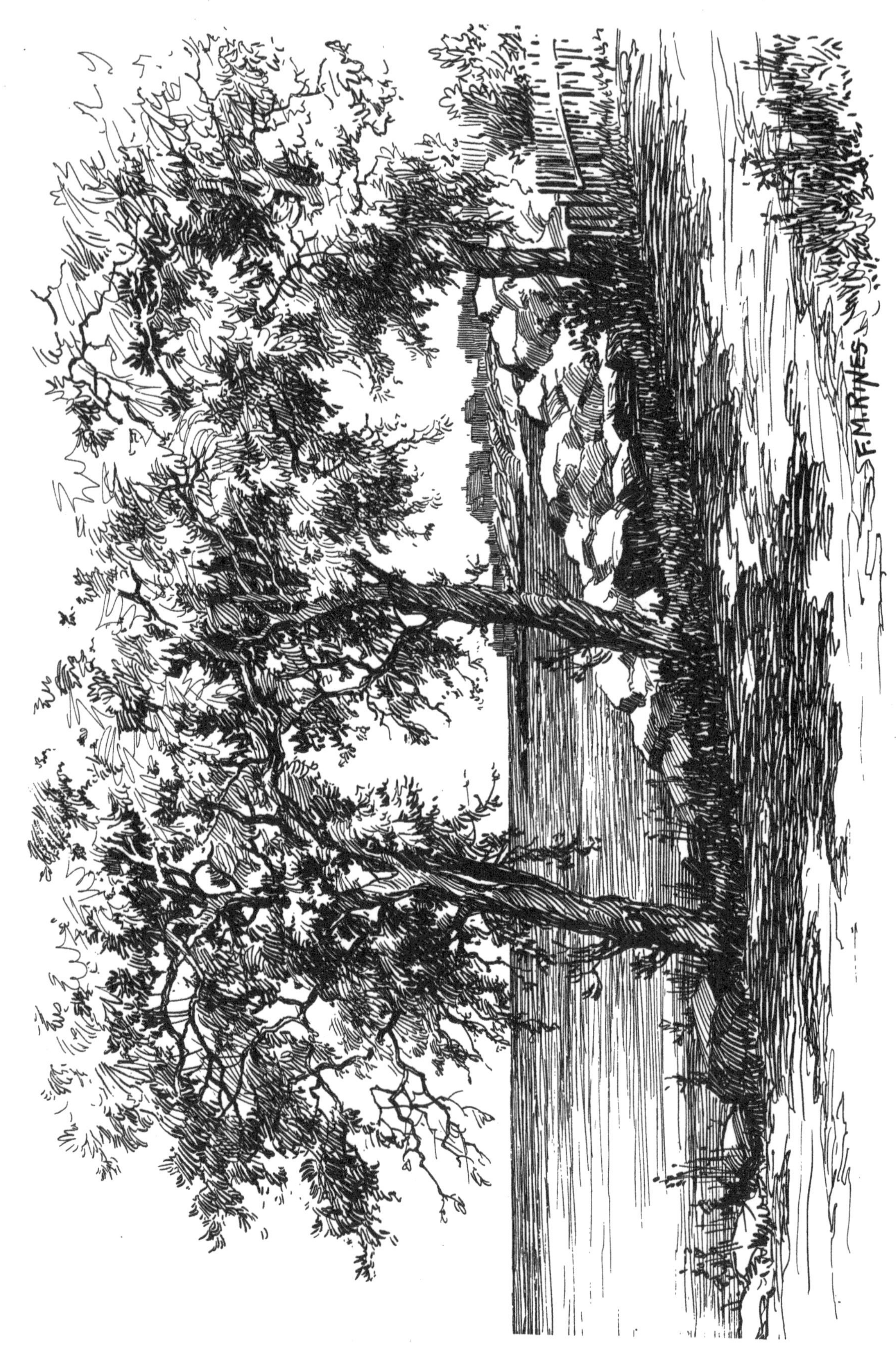

SEASHORE WILLOWS

Medium—Pen and Ink. This drawing presents many of the same problems as those described under the title "Rocks and Willows." It is included partly to emphasize these features more fully and partly to illustrate similarity in handling the two media. While the thought behind the strokes in both instances is the same—i.e. to suggest the direction of growth by the direction of stroke—the result is different, due to the fine pointed instrument in one case and the broader pointed in the other.

The trunks of the trees have been trimmed of their branches for a distance of ten or fifteen feet from the ground, in order to afford passers-by a better view of the water. Nature has done its best to offset this vandalism of man, by sending out new shoots from these cut places. Aided by the naturally gnarled and crooked trunk growth, she has succeeded fairly well—much better than is usually the case with trees which have a straighter and more smoothly growing trunk.

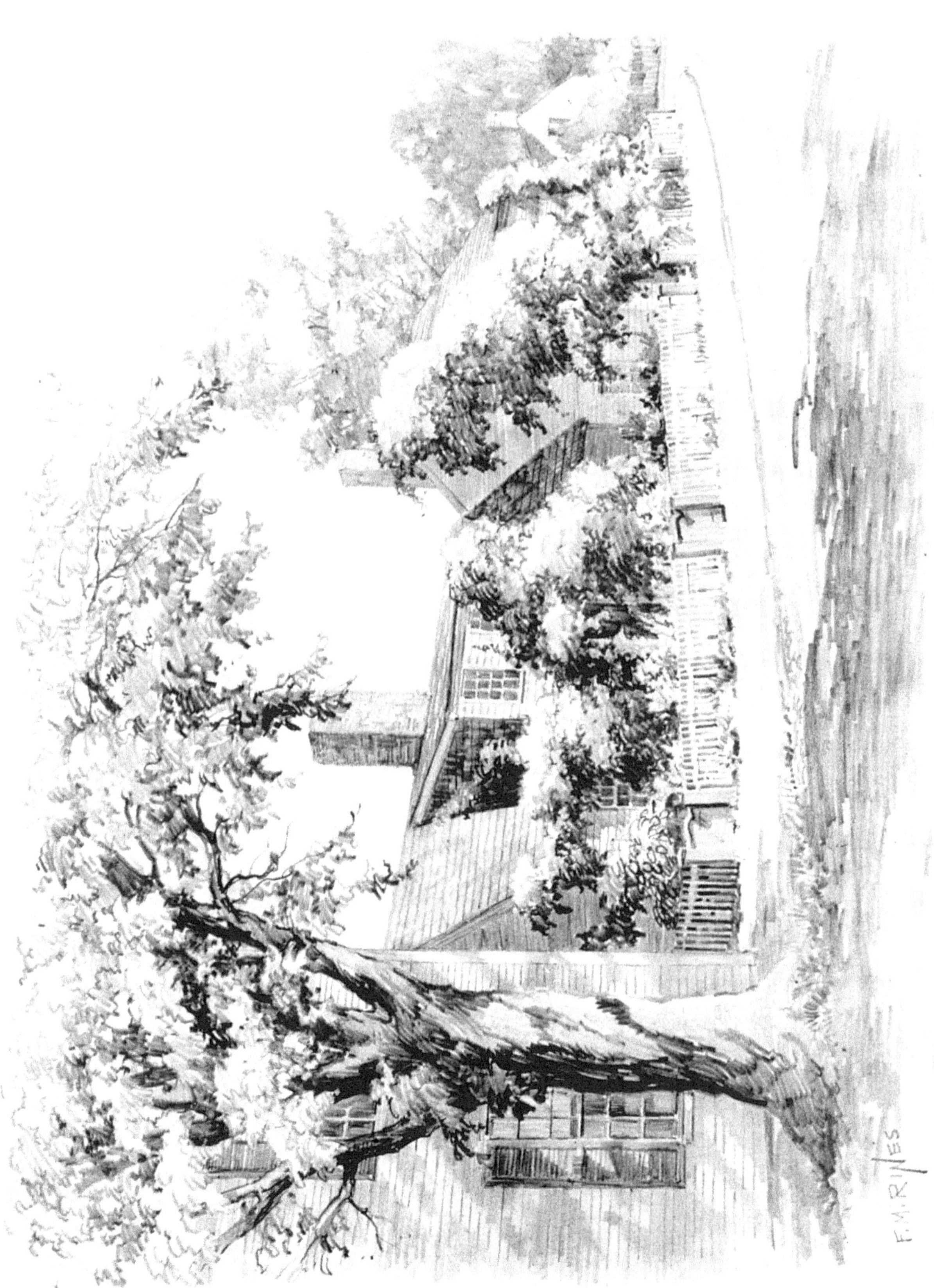

VINE COVERED COTTAGE

Medium—Pencil. This drawing illustrates, among other things, that vines and shrubbery, which are so closely akin to trees, must be drawn (or painted) with the same principles in mind. In one sense, perhaps, they are even more difficult than trees, since very often, as is the case here, there are no twigs or branches to help out the effect. That means that the light and dark masses must be played up to their fullest extent in order to make the drawing interesting. The vine shown in this sketch is heavily massed wisteria.

A suggestion of hollyhocks and other garden flowers behind the fence—not too important in relation to the composition as a whole —is made by simply silhouetting them in white against the dark shadow of the wisteria. Only in a painting could these be emphasized more.

Note the difference in the treatment of the large elm in the foreground and the very much less important maple on the right. The actual elm towered up extremely high before branching out at all. If it had been drawn that way it would have directed the attention out of the picture and would not have been nearly as interesting since it would have appeared as all trunk. This is just one instance where an artist has a great advantage over the photographer.

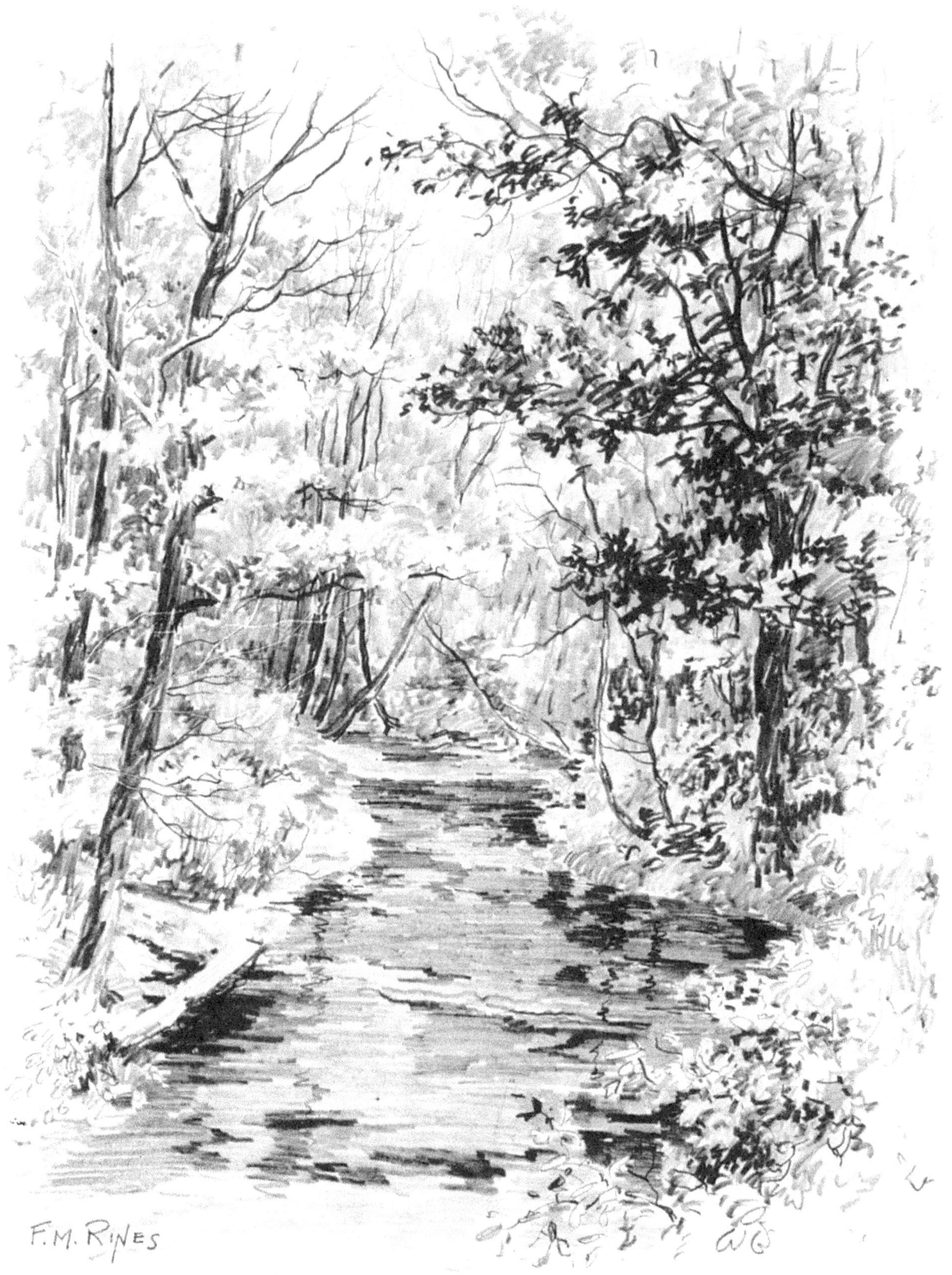
F. M. Rines

TROUT BROOK

Medium—Pencil. Here is a different problem, and an extremely difficult one. Very little individual tree character is distinguishable. The growth happens to be composed of young oaks and maples, interspersed with alders and other shrubs. This fact is of minor importance, however. The important thing to bring out in the drawing is the juxtaposition of light masses against darks, and, vice-versa, the subordination of the background — a series of indefinite, closely valued tones—and the exaggeration of scale in the immediate foreground. All of which is another way of saying that receding planes of the picture must be emphasized as much as possible.

It can readily be seen that no one could possibly draw this scene as it actually appeared. All that can be done is to take certain existing material, discarding nine-tenths of it, and to rearrange or recompose the remainder into an impression of what was there. At the same time, sufficient knowledge of the material must be at hand, so that the observer of the sketch will absorb the idea of an actual flowing stream, the banks of which are choked with trees and undergrowth, instead of thinking that the artist was practicing pencil strokes, or trying out a new set of colors.

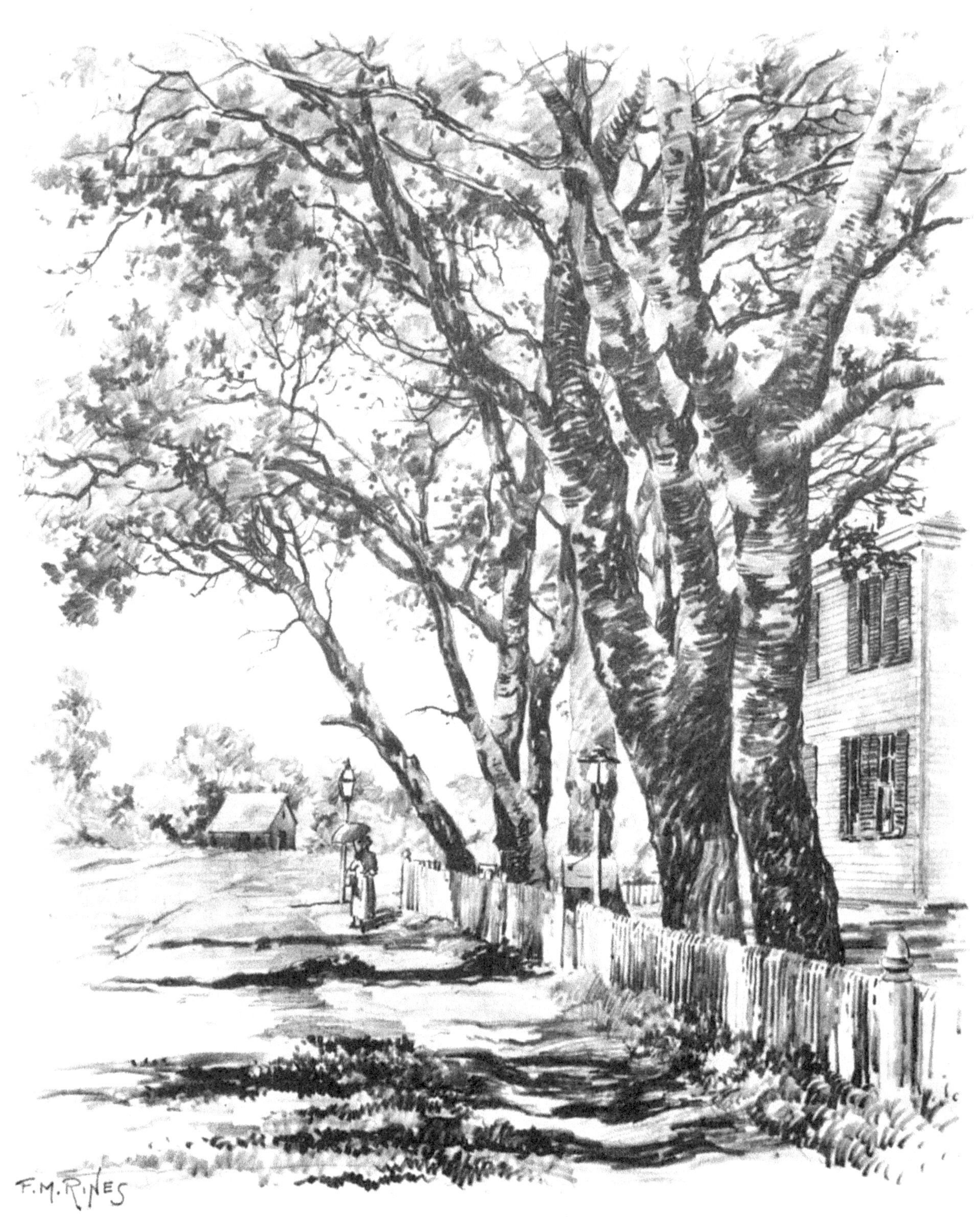
F.M.Rines

SILVER POPLARS

Medium—Pencil. "A Study of Tree Trunks" might be an equally appropriate title for this scene, for the interesting, gnarled trunks are the center of attraction, and the foliage merely serves as a background for them. These trees (which unfortunately space does not admit including in the series of portraits) possess trunks, the bark of which is a peculiar yellow greenish gray in color, mottled with darker gray, or black. This spotting, together with the play of light and shadow cast by the foliage, lends an added interest to what would still be pleasing purely from the viewpoint of growth.

Observe how the direction of the strokes in some places suggests the rounded contour of the trunks, while in other places, in order to avoid monotony, this rounded effect has been ignored.

Consider, in this drawing, as in the others, how important, if unobtrusive, a part the twigs play, in relation to the pattern of the foliage and the sky apertures.

The distant trees have been drawn somewhat stronger in value, with a little more attention to mass forms, than is the case in some of the other sketches. This is because the trunks in the foreground are so very dark and detailed, that this distance can stand more importance. It is entirely a matter of relative values.

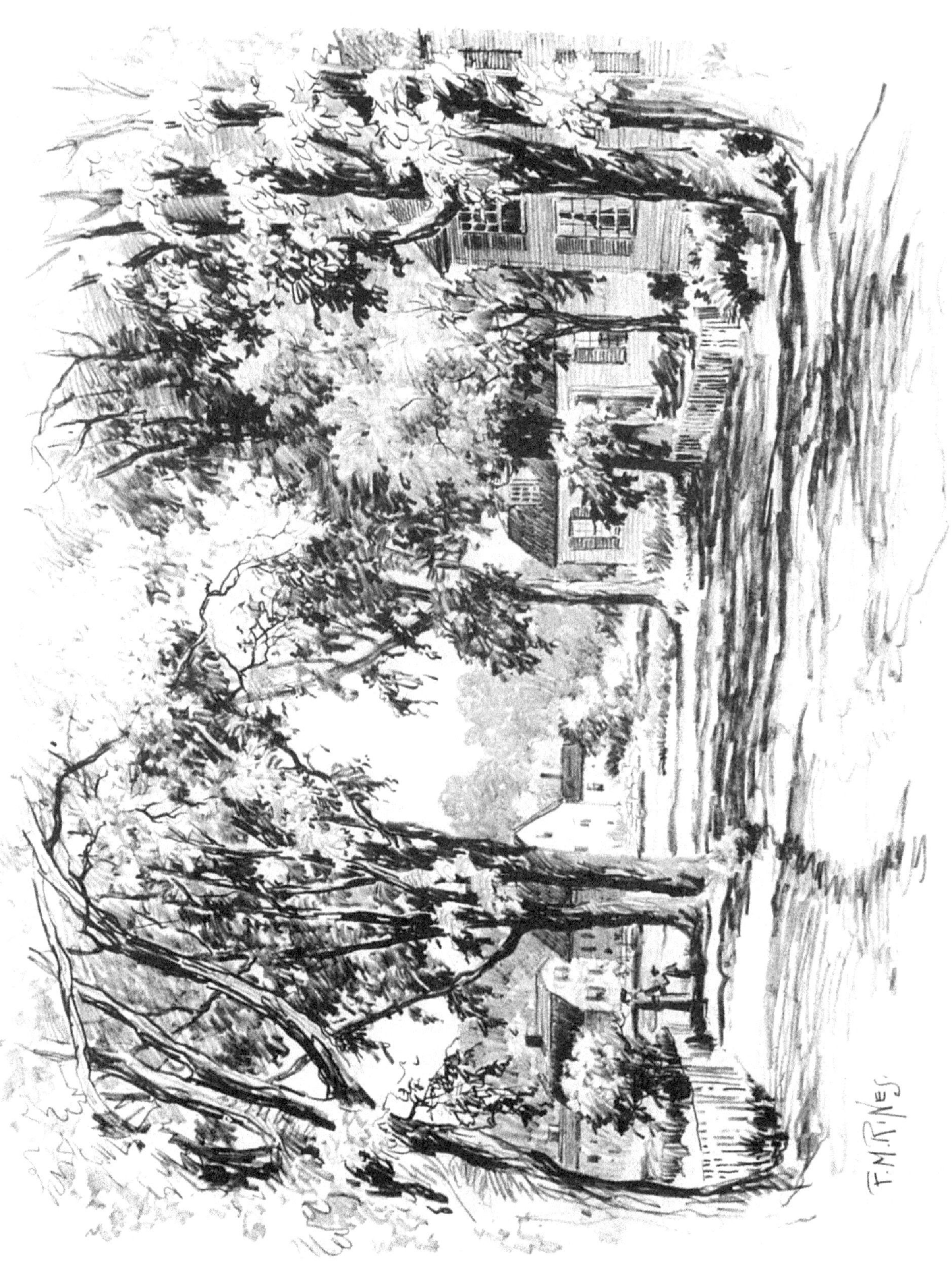

THE EDGE OF THE VILLAGE

Medium—Pencil. The successful rendering of a scene of this nature depends largely upon the treatment of two distinct factors. One is the bringing out of certain details and the subordination of the rest, and the other is the relative spacing of the tree trunks. Of course, these elements enter into every problem of composition to a greater or less extent, but in this particular type their importance is increased.

This double row of old elms could easily appear monotonous if their trunks were spaced at too regular intervals. Their position here is only one of a variety of location which they might occupy. It would be interesting to experiment, by means of some very rough sketches, with various placings of these trunks, in order to prove to yourself just how important this matter of space relation can be.

The very light value of the bunch of foliage on the tree at the extreme left, contrasted with the foliage in deep shadow immediately behind it, and the light, suggested detail of the leaves at the right, bring these two masses into the foreground.

The small tree, between the two houses on the right, while of no particular character by itself, makes an interesting note of contrast in its relation to the other masses.

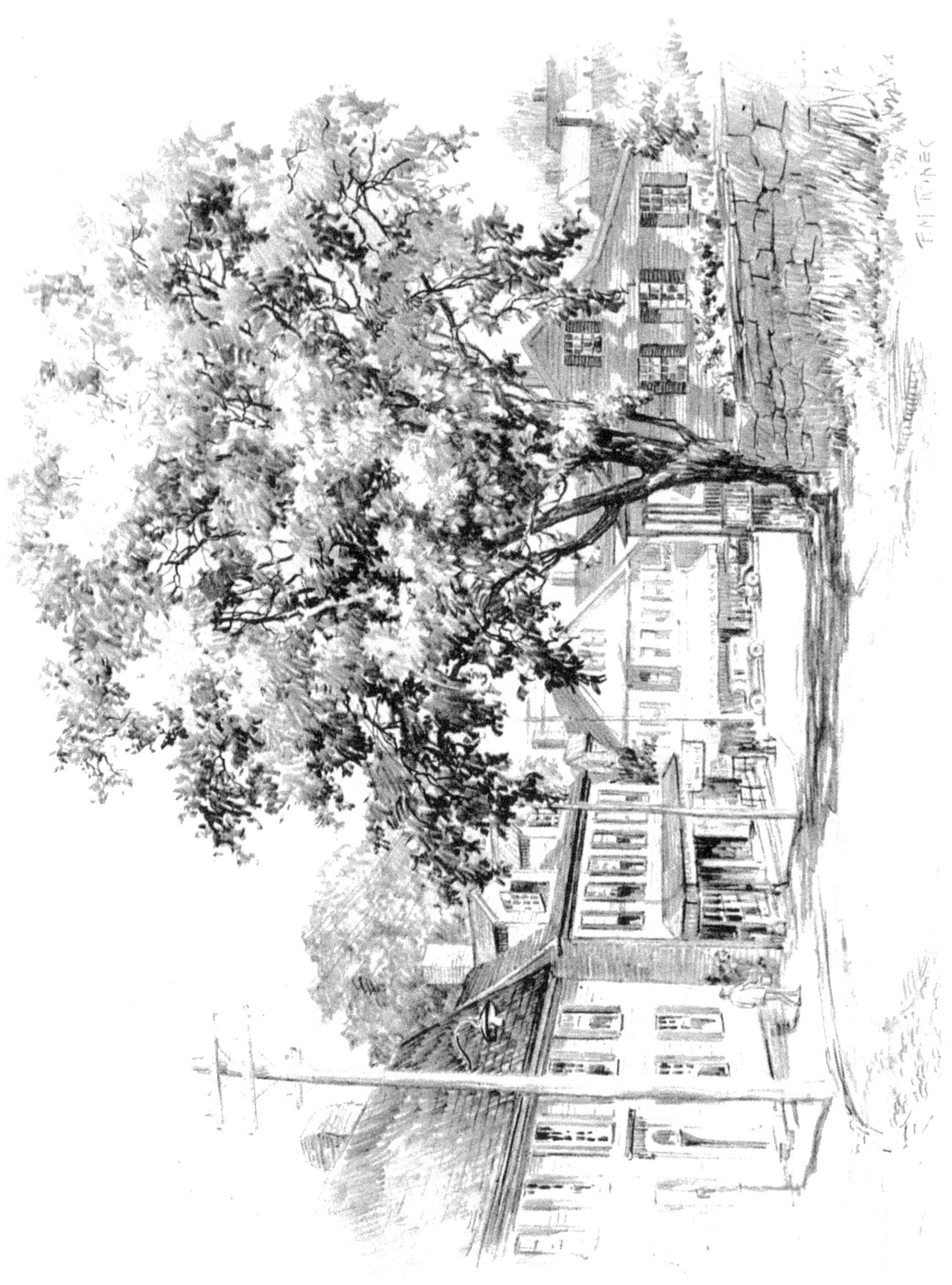

MAIN STREET

Medium—Pencil. Although the title of this drawing definitely puts it into the classification of "street scenes", the elm tree is fully as, if not more, important that the buildings. In fact, the reason for selecting this particular view and angle was because of the tree with its interesting contour standing out so clearly against the sky. Cover up the tree with a piece of paper and see how uninteresting the scene becomes. Now try to imagine any old tree in its place with no particular attention given to either its silhouette or its interior pattern. Try to imagine it rendered all in one tone without the same feeling for sunlight that the houses show. The average photograph would picture it that way, because, as mentioned else-where, the film, unless a filter was used, would not be sufficiently sensitive to the subtle color gradations.

And yet the gradations are there for all to see. It is up to us, as artists, to take advantage of them and to make them interesting. (See last paragraph on page 12.)

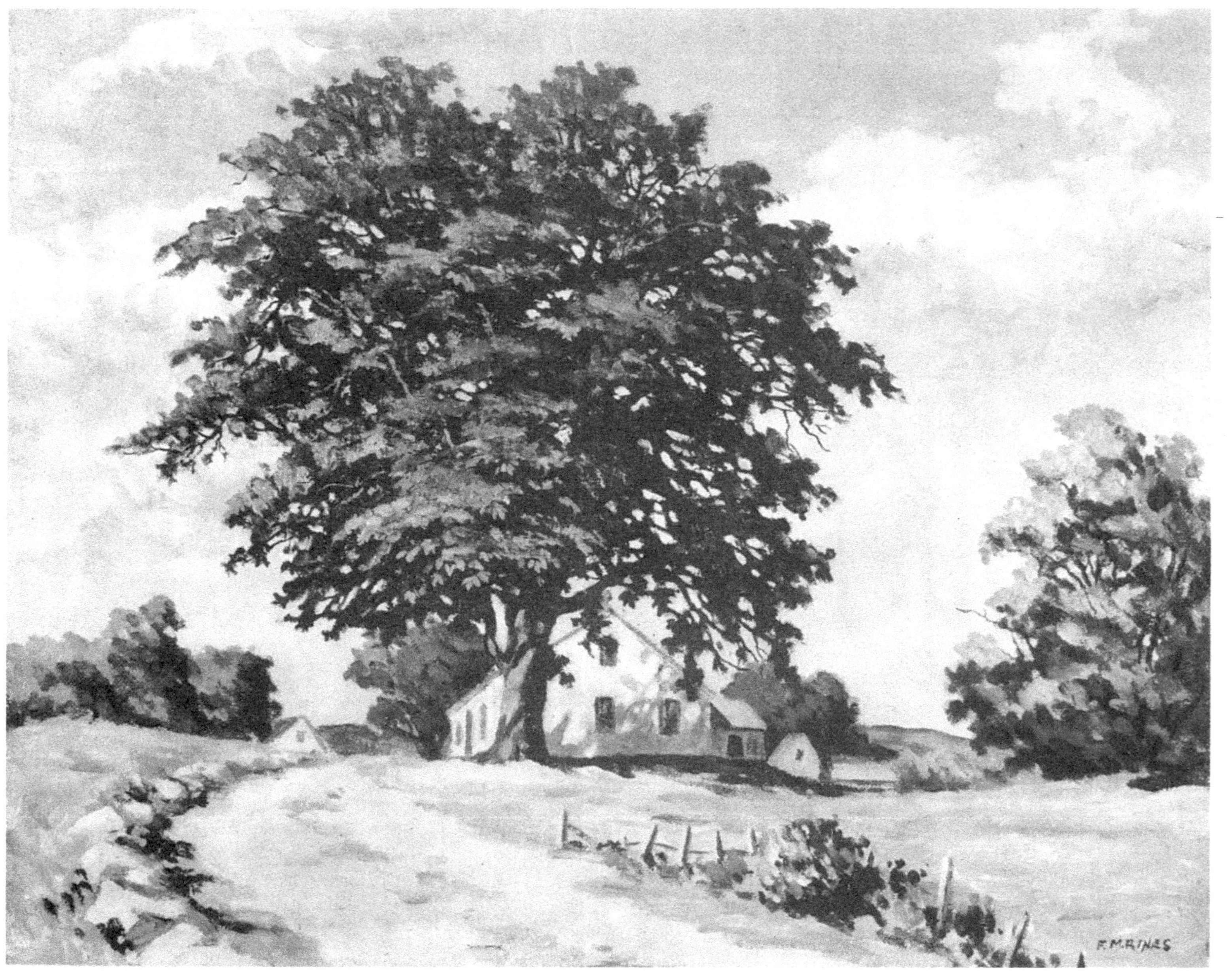

F.M.RINES

HILLTOP FARM

Medium—Oil Paints on Canvas. Here is another elm tree—this time painted instead of drawn. Naturally the effect is somewhat different, yet not nearly as pronounced as some artists would have you believe is necessary. The same attention to first, the pattern of the silhouette and then the pattern or design of the interior masses and the branch structure is as evident here as in the drawings. Even the direction of the brush strokes is governed by the direction of the leaf growth just as the pencil, crayon or pen strokes should be.

To ignore these factors simply because you are using different tools is about as sensible as spelling words differently when writing in longhand or when using a typewriter. Words are words, and trees are trees regardless of how they are presented or represented.

The frontispiece, also painted in oils, is another example of these same principles.

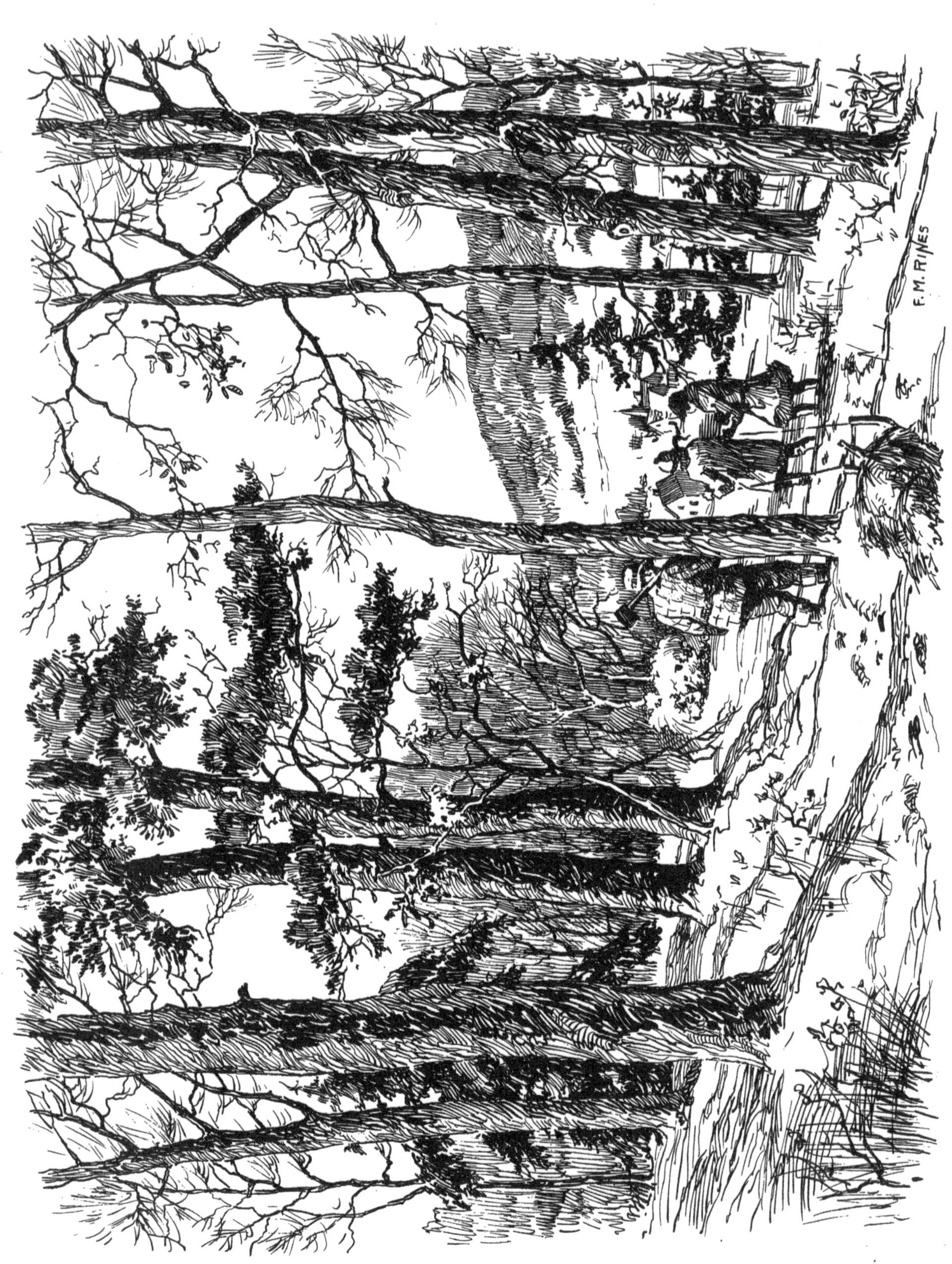

WOODS IN WINTER

Medium—Pen and Ink. Three different kinds of trees are shown in this drawing. The deciduous trees show little resemblance to the oak in the series of tree portraits, yet that is what they are. Their proximity of growth accounts for their straightness and lack of lateral branches. Near the top, if they could be seen, the resemblance would be more evident, as would also the bark texture and foliage. Notice some of the dried leaves still clinging to the twigs. The more exposure to the winds, the less likely are these leaves to remain on the tree.

The two large trees, to the left of the center, are distinctly pines. Their horizontal branches and upward growing foliage are easily recognizable. In contrast to these are the drooping branches and the foliage beneath the limbs, on the spruce tree, behind the large trunk at the left, and also on those over the brow of the hill, on the right.

The mass of bare trees in the left middle distance is handled with a stroke *suggesting* the growth, with a nearer tree or two in sufficient detail to relieve the monotony.

Designing the sky spaces—breaking them up with branches here and there—should be given as much thought in a scene like this as when drawing an individual tree.